Praise for Carlos Dews's *Hush*

"Interweaving several narrative lines, Carlos Dews has fashioned a raw, suspenseful autobiographical narrative. His prose is clear and steady, one sentence after another pulling the reader forward and down deeper into many overlapping raw, eye-opening stories of human survival. *Hush* has a gripping, mesmerizing power that will bring you in and not let you go."

> — **Billy Collins**, U.S. Poet Laureate (2001-2003) and
> author of *The Rain in Portugal* (Random House, 2016).

"*Hush* is a book that builds new neighborhoods in your heart. Children never forgetting, autofiction playing Helter Skelter with history, and love like diamond-encrusted mud everywhere you step: watch out or life will turn into a gun that eats you, which is the precise power of Dews's literary homage to fear, family, and indeed the future. What are we without our unforgettings? *Hush* is a roadmap for all who care to travel to their own places of haunting, and come out the other side well-companioned and wiser. This is a book for every month of the year, including the month that time forgot."

> — **Susan Bradley Smith**, Author of the verse novels
> *Gladland*, and *The Postcult Heart*, and the memoir
> *Friday Forever*, Professor of Creative Writing at Curtin
> University, Australia.

"*Hush* is a deeply felt, tightly plotted tale of generations of cruel men and their suffering wives, living in hardscrabble poverty—an instant classic! Stark as the portraits might be, they are always rendered with compassion. Dews has a heart as big as Texas."

> — **Edmund White**, author of *A Boy's Own Story* and
> *A Saint From Texas.*

"An elegiac and open-hearted ride through three generations of a working-class Texas family. This is an emotional and moving story of violence and limitation in which women are controlled, either directly or through social expectation, and men always have a place to turn to. Carlos Dews defies nostalgia in this reimagining of classic American tropes."

— **Sarah Schulman**, author of *The Cosmopolitans*.

"If Robert Altman had ever gone down to East Texas, he couldn't have portrayed the cacophonous and diverse journey of the Dews family with any more veracity, harsh honesty, or grit. In this brilliant fictionalized account of a lineage hardened by poverty, bias, domestic violence, mental illness, migrations, unlikely births and deaths—with visitations of indefatigable belief and goodheartedness—Carlos Dews makes of the spare, understated language of his people a mosaic, a single story composed from all the broken parts. *Hush* is a masterpiece."

— **David Keplinger**, author of *Another City* (2018)
and *The Long Answer: New and Selected Poems* (2020)

"Generations tied to the land, twisted by cycles of subsistence and the harsh realities of passion and abuse, Carlos Dews's characters are rugged woodcut figures out of Dürer."

— **Michael Carroll**, winner of the Sue Kaufman
Prize for first fiction from the American Academy of
Arts and Letters for *Little Reef and Other Stories*.

"Sad country songs, reports on cattle prices, and the rare local news. This is what we hear on the car radio while driving through East Texas in *Hush*—but just wait. Dews tells a 'story of his own' by weaving rural Southern folklife and lore into the family history of the Scogins and Dews up on Fitzy Junction in Nacogdoches, Texas, where wisteria vines climb in heart pine woods, cornbread soaks in buttermilk, and the only son of an only son of an only son daydreams beneath 'a field of fabric.'"

—**Alex Gregor**, author of *The Pollen Path* (Radioactive
Cloud, 2019)

HUSH

A FICTION

Carlos Dews

Negative Capability PRESS

MOBILE ALABAMA

Hush

Cover Illustration by Jean Fitzgerald
Book Design by Jenni Krchak

ISBN 978-0-9986777-6-7
Library of Congress Control Number: 2020932321

Negative Capability Press
150 Du Rhu Drive, #2202
Mobile, Alabama 36608
(251)591-2922

www.negativecapabilitypress.org
facebook.com/negativecapabilitypress

ACKNOWLEDGMENTS

For being there from the beginning and supporting me along the way, I thank Eduardo Luis Leon, William Lamar Polk III, and Steven Estok.

From my days at the New School University, where I wrote the first words of *Hush*, I'd like to thank Stephen Serwin, Steven Estok (again), Andrew Cotto, Jackson Taylor, Frederic Tuten, Dale Peck, and Patrick McGrath.

Thanks to Jenni Krchak for designing the book, inside and out. Thanks to Sue Walker for believing in *Hush* when no one else seemed to. And thanks to Jean Fitzgerald for first learning what a dog trot was then drawing one.

Thanks to all my colleagues at John Cabot University in Rome, Italy, who have, over the years, endured perhaps one too many readings of the sections of *Hush* in progress. And thanks to John Cabot University's Faculty Development Committee and President Franco Pavoncello and Dean Mary Merva for the award of a sabbatical that allowed me to complete *Hush*, at last.

Thanks to Bill Guion, a fellow Texan, for sharing with me the streets of Rome. Thanks to James Mayo and Carolyn Leste Law for forever being my friends. And thanks to Bret Pearson for being the first to tell me that these stories mattered.

Thanks to the people of Buenos Aires, Argentina; Erongaricuaro, Mexico; Calcata, Rome, Vasto, Monteprandone, and San Benedetto del Tronto, Italy; Sigri, Greece; Assagao, Goa, India; and Kuwait City, Kuwait, for the space and time to write parts of *Hush* while among them.

And thanks to Sarah Forbes Dews, Mildred Scogin Dews, Fusako

Terao Scogin, and Lois Minter Dews, for their stories, and for allowing me to invent new ones for them.

And for arriving, at long last, but now forever, I thank Antonino Colapinto.

"Children don't forget. Children don't forget."
— Virginia Woolf, *To the Lighthouse*

1945

Fusako walked, her shoulders hunched and her eyes cast down. She looked only far enough ahead to avoid the obstacles in her path along the road. She didn't want to see anything that stood between her and her destination. Too many reminders, too many calls for help. And she knew she had so far to walk that seeing into the distance would only discourage her. She didn't have any other choice, no other place to go.

With each step the words of her parents echoed in her ears. "If anything should happen to us, if after the war or when our work is done, you can't find us, make your way to Doctor Ito's house. He and his wife will look after you until we can make it there. They live in Kurume. Follow the road along the river. Walk with the river. It will take you to them. Do not cross a bridge, follow the water. Doctor Ito and his wife should be safe, no matter what happens with the war. Make your way to them. Don't forget."

They had repeated these words to her when they left her at the school six months before, her father returning to the city and his war job and her mother, always at his side, refusing to evacuate the city when all those not required for the war effort were forced to leave Nagasaki. Her two brothers were to remain in the city as well, working in the same factory as their father.

She held in her hand the strap of a small cloth bag. It hung near-ly to the ground, swinging with each step. It held her school uniform and a single pair of extra shoes. She was wearing the clothes she wore the day she arrived at the school, much too warm for August. Western dress. A white collared shirt, brown jacket and brown skirt. She wore thick, white wool socks, and a hat that matched her skirt. A black coat covered her shoulders.

Although only two days had passed since they received word at the school about the giant American bomb, Fusako couldn't tell if her vision of the blast came to her in a dream the following night or if it was the image she had created in her mind as she walked. She kept recalling the words the school's headmaster used to describe the bomb's destruction.

The entire city. The entire city, he kept saying. As if he thought the girls were unable to comprehend a single power in the world that could be capable of such an act.

All gone. All gone. The entire city. All gone.

It took further insistence on the part of the headmaster to over-come Fusako's denial that everything she knew had been destroyed. Her parents, her brothers, their house, her former school, the facto-ry where her father and brothers worked, the shops along the street where her mother bought fish and rice and tea, perhaps even all her friends. In response to her speculation that her family had decided to take a trip into the countryside and might have survived, the headmaster told her that the bomb had fallen at nine in the morn-ing and that with the war effort and the necessity of the factories to continue their work apace, not to mention the shortage of coal and diesel and wood, all unnecessary travel had been forbidden. He reminded her of the difficulty that they had had in bringing her out of the city to school. And things were much more difficult now.

They had kept the news of the bombs from the girls as best they could, but when one of them heard two of the maids talking of the huge number of dead, the administration first tried to determine the fate of the families of the girls from the two cities before telling them the truth.

The headmaster learned that there was no news and little hope for the family of Fusako Terao. Her father and brothers worked in the steel factory along the waterfront and the family home was less than half a mile away, in an old central neighborhood—both well within the range of the heaviest damage. Total destruction, absolutely no survivors, no hope of it, as the officer had explained to the headmaster.

The matron of the school had offered to allow Fusako to stay with her, along with some of the other girls, until something could be done, but that was not what her parents had told her. Find Doctor Ito. He will know what to do.

She left school the following morning without saying a word, without telling anyone, not even her friends. She walked through the gates at the front of her school, asked for directions to the river, and joined the throngs along the way.

Fusako had only traveled between Nagasaki and Hita, passing through Kurume, by train, and had no idea how many days it would take to walk between the cities. Every time the road veered from the riverbank and she lost sight of the water, she would pause and ask the next person she saw if they knew the way. In towns that had train stations she would ask if the trains were running and if she could buy a ticket to Kurume, but the answer was always the same. Unlike many of the people on the road, Fusako at least had money to make her way tolerable. She had taken all her own savings and the money her parents had given her for emergency use and now spent it bit by bit, for meals when she was hungry or a place to sleep at night. She felt invisible, as if everyone else was so concerned with their own difficulties that they couldn't see the young girl of thirteen traveling alone.

On the third day of her walk, just as Fusako entered yet another small town, a strap on one of her shoes broke. She sat down on a large rock at the side of the road and picked up the shoe, holding it in front of her face. The tiny leather strap across the top of her foot had snapped next to the silver buckle.

She began to cry. This loss, this final tiny loss, minute in comparison to the accumulated losses of only three days before, opened her up, forced her to face her place in the world. Tears united beneath her chin, dripping on the front of her jacket. She held the sides of her head in her hands and closed her eyes. She heard a temple bell from the center of the town and her ears began to note the other sounds around her. Voices. The sounds of movement. She heard the whispers between two old women as they passed in front of her. The war is over. Humiliation. The Emperor's voice on the radio. The war was over. What would happen next?

Fusako opened her eyes and looked up the street, following the two women as they disappeared into the growing, anxious crowd coming into the narrow main street. All her patience and resignation left her. She was now afraid and alone.

She opened her bag and slipped on her other pair of shoes, brought the broken shoe together with its mate, and placed them on the ground behind the rock on which she sat. She wanted to run the rest of the way to Kurume, to find the safety of Doctor Ito's house, to drink tea, to eat sweets, to be a child and forget what had happened.

1903

Sarah stood beside the wash pot behind the house, stirring in the soap with a wooden paddle as the water reached a boil. She heard a squeal and thud. She spun around, looked onto the back porch and saw the baby still asleep on the pallet where she had left her.

"Boys?"

Carlos ran around the corner of the house.

"Momma, Pablo fell off old Blue and hurt his head."

Sarah dropped the paddle against the rim of the kettle and followed her son to the side of the house.

Pablo's shoulder seemed to disappear into the soft ground where he had fallen. His arm extended above his head, as if he had tried to break the fall. His legs were parted and his bare feet were twisted into tortured angles.

She knew he was dead when she saw him.

The edge of the two-faced ax was in the ground next to the stump where she had left it after splitting the wood for the wash fire. The upper edge of the ax entered his head where his hair met his forehead, just above his left eye. Blood streamed down the blade of the ax and pooled on the ground.

Sarah ran to Pablo's side. "Go get your papa."

Carlos ran to the barn and returned with his father.

"Papa, we was just trying to ride Blue together. He bucked and Pablo fell off."

His father raised his hand back toward his son. Carlos stopped. He knew not to say another word.

Sarah turned to her husband, her son in her arms, the bloodied ax at her knees. "Frank. He's gone."

The mule stood grazing on a tuft of grass that grew at the edge of the house. Frank walked to the mule, shoving its shoulder with the broad palm of his hand to free one of the reins on which it stood. He gathered both reins in his hand and led the mule to the plank wood fence that bordered the yard.

Frank tied the mule's head up short. There was only a foot of rope between the top rung of the fence and the bit in the mule's mouth. He walked to his wife and son, lifted the ax and walked back toward the mule.

Sarah followed him with her eyes. "Frank, don't."

He began by hitting the mule with the flat face of the ax, tearing the skin over its hip bone. The mule made a high-pitched squeal that seemed to ask a question. It stomped its heavy hooves to avoid the next blow. Frank cursed with each swing as he brought down the ax. The animal lurched back, trying to free its head from the bridle. Frank took a single step to the right and continued.

Carlos squinted when the sunlight reflected off the ax as the iron head reached the pinnacle of its swing. Frank pulled it down with all his weight, dragging the sharp edge through the air toward the mule's backbone.

It took one more swing to bring the mule to its knees, two more still to get it broadside on the ground, its head pulled upward by the reins still tied to the fence. The final blow, just above its shoulders, stopped the labored breathing. Before he stepped away, Frank untied the reins. The mule's head slopped to the ground. Its lips slipped shut, covering the bit and the bloody teeth.

"Boy, take that bridle off and put it in the shed."

Frank turned away from the mule's body. His wife still sat on the ground, their dead son in her arms, her dress and apron soaked in blood. Wood chips from the ground around the chopping stump stuck to her and the dead boy. She sat cross-legged, rocking back and forth, Pablo's bare feet on the ground near her knees, the boy's head pressed against the flat comfort above her left breast. She had already closed his eyes.

His chin rested close to his chest, as if in prayer. His tongue protruded between his teeth. His mother's lips hovered just above the even gash on the side of his head, her lips moving closer with each rock, as if poised to give the wound a reluctant kiss.

February 1950

Fusako kept the door to Doctor Ito's office open to encourage the patients to find her at the end of the long hallway. Doctor Ito insisted that she wear her white coat whenever she worked behind the reception desk, just like the nurses. He said it made a good impression on the patients and that, although she wasn't yet a nurse herself, it made people think of her as one. Doctor Ito took his role as her foster father seriously. He had known her father since they were both school boys in Nagasaki. He and his wife were childless, so when she arrived on their doorstep within a week of the death of her entire family, they were happy to take her in.

Fusako sat behind the reception desk, at the end of the long hallway that led from the street beside the doctor's consulting room back to the reception area. She was always distracted when someone walked by the open door at the street and temporarily blocked out the bright sunlight. Fusako was especially attuned to seeing those too timid or scared to walk into the office for their appointments. There was something about how the color of their uniforms changed the light at the end of the hallway that identified them for her. The American soldiers always walked back and forth in front of the doorway before they could muster the courage to walk down the hall and ask to see the doctor for their injections. Doctor Ito told her he was amazed at how quickly the soldiers had learned that he was more than willing to administer a shot of penicillin and prevent them from facing the wrath, then obligatory lecture, from the Army doctors and their commanding officers.

Doctor Ito spoke English, the only doctor in town who could, so the soldiers could describe their symptoms to him before he asked them to lower their trousers and gave them the required injection. The soldiers paid for his services with food supplies. Doctor Ito didn't keep any records for the soldiers, so Fusako didn't have to ask for their names. She just pointed at an empty seat in the waiting area and said "wait for doctor, wait for doctor," one of the few expressions the doctor had taught her to use with the soldiers. She directed them into the consulting room once the previous patient left through the side door and Doctor Ito rang a bell.

Beyond seeing them walking down the streets in threes and fours or driving down the narrow streets in their trucks and jeeps, this was her only interaction with the Americans. She divided them into various categories depending on the way they interacted with her when they came in for their shots. Some barked at her, storming toward her desk with their loud boots shaking the entire wood building. As if they were already familiar with her, as if she spoke English, as if they were angry with her or blamed her for the problems that brought them to her desk. Others seemed to regard her as they would a schoolmaster or a very stern parent, beginning to bow as they walked down the hallway and continuing to do so nervously throughout their exchange. Still others behaved like little brothers, familiar and sweet, wanting to chat and smile even though little was communicated between them. And then there were those who felt that she was a Japanese doll, like the ones they bought in the market to send home to wives or mothers or sisters, with a painted white face, wearing a traditional robe, and willing to provide them with any pleasure they desired. Fusako wished that her countrywomen wouldn't do just that, so the soldiers wouldn't think all Japanese women did the same.

Fusako looked at the clock on the wall opposite her desk and wondered if he would return at the same time for the fifth day. At exactly three in the afternoon for the last four days, an American soldier had stood directly across the street, opposite the door of Doctor Ito's office. He stayed there for the final two hours of Fusako's workday, only turning to walk away when she closed the door at the street to patients and returned to her desk to close the office for the day. But he was always gone when she left the office for the short walk to the house where she lived with Doctor Ito.

She would have been scared if any other soldier had behaved in this way. But there was something about this soldier's face that assured her his intentions were kind. She decided, after the third day, he was not just a soldier too shy to enter the door and walk down the hallway to see Doctor Ito for treatment. This soldier was there to see her.

And she had seen him before. They met on the sidewalk when she was walking to work one morning. She usually walked with her eyes at her feet, especially when there were soldiers in the street, but an unusual sound had lifted her eyes for a second and she met the gaze of the soldier. He was wearing his dress uniform. When their eyes met as they came close to one another on the narrow sidewalk, he tipped his hat, nodded his head and smiled.

This American soldier was different. Not different from her, which he certainly was, but not the same as all the other American soldiers she had seen. She recognized tenderness in his eyes. Something unlike the tightened faces and raised chins of most of the soldiers she saw walking in the city. The others seemed to walk around as giants, moving their arms and legs beyond the space they needed to carry them from place to place. They walked as if the world and all its space had been made just for their use. Their knees moved to the sides and they opened their thighs as they walked. Their elbows flew and their shoulders swayed from left to right as they walked.

Not this soldier. Although his uniform seemed to fit him properly, there was something about the way he held himself, the way his body moved within his uniform, that made her think he didn't feel

worthy of it. He moved nervously, quickly, as if he expected a heavy
weight to fall from the sky on him at any moment. And he was always adjusting his uniform. Removing and replacing his hat, pulling at his collar as if he were hot even on the coolest day. He always
pulled down on the tail of his jacket, when he wore one, or tucked
in his shirt and adjusted his tie. And his shoulders; he could sustain
the posture that Fusako knew the soldiers were taught for only a few
seconds at a time before his shoulders would move forward and a
small hump would appear on his back between his shoulders. Fusako thought it looked as if he had a rope around his waist and he was
pulling a heavy weight behind him. He leaned forward slightly and
mostly looked toward the ground when he walked. With cheekbones
that protruded just beneath his eyes, he looked hungry and vulnerable and his eyes appeared as if he were on the verge of crying.

But she liked his unusual, boyish, sad face. She told herself as
he walked away at the end of his hours on the fourth day that, if he
returned a fifth time, she would speak to him.

Yet Fusako knew what it meant to be seen with an American soldier. She knew what a sacrifice she would be making. She would be
a whore.

At exactly three in the afternoon, he appeared opposite the en-
trance to the office then leaned against the wall across the street.
Fusako continued her afternoon work, glancing up from her desk to
see if he still stood against the wall. Each time she looked at his face
and their eyes met, he looked down at his boots or pretended to see
something of interest down the street.

She could not imagine what she would say to this soldier. Did he
speak Japanese? Her own English would not allow for a conversation.

She looked down the hall to see him smile as she began to close
the office. She removed her white coat and hung it on the peg behind her desk. She walked to the end of the hall to close the door,
as she had done the previous four days. Before she knew what she
was doing, she nodded her head and stepped aside, making a space
inside the doorway for him to fill. He looked up and down the street

then rushed across and into the door. She closed the door behind him and they faced each other across the narrow hallway—their backs pressed against its opposite walls.

"Hiddee."

She looked up into his face, smiled, then looked straight ahead at how his tie was tucked into his shirt below the second button. She said nothing in response.

"Do you speak English?"

"A little."

"I don't know what to say to you. You sure are a pretty little thing. And mighty sweet looking."

She looked back up at his face. "Hello. This way, please." She used a few of the only words she knew of his language and pointed back down the hallway toward the small waiting room and her desk. He didn't move.

"No, Mam. That's just fine. I'm not here to see the doctor. I just wanted to say hello and see if you might want to see me another time. Away from here."

She understood hello and another time from her dealings with the soldiers. She nodded.

"Good. Thank you, Mam. I'll come back tomorrow." He bowed his head and lifted his hat from his side to his chest. "My name is Weldon. Sergeant David Weldon Scogin."

"My name is Fusako."

"Fusako. Fusako. That's a pretty name."

1908

Carlos woke as if from a bad dream. The quilt on his sister's side of the bed was turned back in a perfect triangle. The sheet next to him was cold. He sat up and searched for the sound that woke him. But the room, only a few steps square, was quiet. Maybe another mad dog had come onto the porch or the dogs had chased a skunk under the house. Or their mother had run away again.

He sat on the edge of the bed, his legs framed in a faint rectangle of moonlight that streamed through the window.

Hurried footsteps across the hallway. A chair's complaint against the plank floor. A struggle. The opening of the door to his parents' room down the dogtrot hallway. His mother's voice. His father's voice, louder.

The door to his room opened, his mother's hand on the ceramic knob.

"My babies!"

It was all she said before his father grabbed her wrist and pulled her hand off the knob. The door slammed. Something heavy dropped onto the floor in the dogtrot. He heard the quick tread of his mother down the wood steps of the front porch, a curse from his father.

Carlos ran to the door and opened it. He looked down the

hallway toward the porch and saw his mother rush into the field across the road from the house. His father sat on the steps pulling on his boots, thumbing the straps of his overalls onto his shoulders. He stood and ran after his wife.

Carlos stepped into the hallway, his foot hitting the wooden handle of the ax they used to chop wood for the stove. He picked it up just behind its iron head and leaned it against the wall of the broad hallway.

He stood on the weathered planks of the porch, feeling the grit from the field and the grain of the worn wood on the soles of his bare feet. His nightshirt brushed the back of his knees as the breeze blew through the dogtrot.

His mother ran across the newly plowed field. Her white cotton nightgown glowed in the moonlight, flitting like a lightning bug, zigzagging across the rows. Her black hair and brown skin disappeared against the soil, leaving only the dancing ghost of her shift. She tripped in a furrow and fell against the damp earth.

"Carlos, where's Momma?"

Cordelia stood at his side, pulling at his nightshirt.

"She's run off again but Papa's gone to get her. Get back in the bed."

The girl turned and walked back down the dogtrot.

Their mother reached the spine of a ridge that ran across the field. The other side sloped to the creek that marked the boundary of the land they worked. She was silent but the boy could hear his father shouting as he chased her. "Sarah, I'm telling you, you better git back here. Don't you make me catch you."

She ran down the opposite side of the hill. To Carlos, it looked as if the hill swallowed her. The last he saw of his mother was a snip of white fabric, her shoulder briefly lifting above the crest of the hill then sinking back down beneath it, as she took a frantic stride toward the creek.

Two years before, when they fled the Indian Territory and left her people behind, Sarah Dews had insisted that the family settle among trees. Her people had been forced from the forest-covered hills of Alabama long before she was born. And although she had never seen those Eastern woods, she preferred them to the flat, grassy land of Oklahoma. When, during their move to Texas, Frank showed her a farm along the Trinity River just south of Dallas, she surveyed the fields and the sparse trees and shook her head. She did not want to be able to see a horizon and she wanted to smell rotting leaves. They continued on to the south and east.

Frank's temper was the reason they had to leave Oklahoma. An Indian man, a distant cousin of Sarah, lay dying in the road just outside the farm where she had been born. Frank had beaten the man unconscious over nothing in particular. After the fight, Frank yelled for Sarah to get their things together and pile them into the wagon. He grabbed the tack and feed from the shed next to the house and hitched up their one mule. They put Carlos and Cordelia on top of the heap in the bed of the wagon and fled. The man's blood was still flowing next to the road as they drove away from Oklahoma toward Texas.

After a week of sleeping under the bed of the wagon, wandering southward and eastward from the Indian Territory, they found themselves on a narrow sand road in East Texas. In the center of a field carved out of the surrounding stands of pine and hardwood trees, Frank spotted an empty shell of a house with a barn to its side.

The house was built on pilings of red rocks gathered from the nearby woods. It was gray and weathered. With a chimney at each end and a shingled wood roof, it had never been painted. Porches stretched across the front and back, and its two rooms, with two windows each, were divided by an open-air hallway. They called the hallway a dogtrot. The barn sat to the side and just behind the house.

A black boy leading a mule toward them down the road told them that the place belonged to a Mister Williams who lived in a big white house out on the main road.

By the end of that day, Frank Dews had convinced the owner to let them move into the house and farm the fields around it. Mister

Williams would front the money for expenses. After that was paid back, Frank would receive one half of any profits from the sale of the cotton or any other crops they grew on Mister Williams's land. He called it farming on the halves.

Mister Williams owned everything in sight. The house, the bucket they used to draw their water, the well behind the house, the water down below, the grass, the very soil they worked, and even the deer that sometimes slipped out of the pine woods into the edge of the fields. The entire family worked every day to tease out as much cotton as they could from the sandy soil. They grew vegetables in a small patch at the side of the house and milked a cow borrowed from Mister Williams's herd.

The only improvement Mister Williams made to the house was the addition of glass in the four windows, paid for with an advance against the sale of their first crop. Sarah sewed curtains out of feed sacks for the windows that faced the road and kept the yard in front and behind the house scraped clean, raked, and packed as hard as stone.

They did not know the name of the county where they had settled until they had lived there three months. Frank heard it at the cotton gin where he had gone to buy seed for the spring planting. He said it over and over to himself all afternoon so he could repeat it to his wife that night. He thought it sounded like one of the words her people used when they whispered to each other in their own language, when he was certain they were talking about him. Naka-doe-chez, Naka-doe-chez. Nacogdoches.

He caught her as she left the field. She tripped on the blackberry vines that grew along the path of a rail fence long gone. Her right temple hit the ground first, then her elbow and hip. He was on her before she could get up. He shoved his knee in the valley of her back and pushed her face into the ground.

He pulled a short length of narrow jute rope from his back pocket, doubled it, and wrapped it around her neck.

"Bitch, I told you not to run." He held the ends at the back of her neck and stood up. "This is it for you."

She tried to stand but lost her balance, the rope tearing at the skin of her neck. He pulled her along for three strides, grunting with each step, as she slid along the ground behind him. She managed to bring her feet under herself and stand.

"You'll never run from me again."

She tried to speak but the rope tightened.

"This is it for you."

He led her to the stand of willow trees that grew along the bank of the creek, pushed her back against the trunk of a sapling, removed the rope from her neck, and tied her hands behind the tree.

"This was your last time doing this. What did you think you could do with that ax?"

He stood in front of her and looked down into her eyes.

"If you holler for help, even a little bit, I'll come right back down here and drown you in that creek."

He turned and walked back toward the house.

She bent her knees and slipped down the trunk until she sat on the cold wet ground. With every movement of her body the branches above her head rustled as the thin willows made contact with their neighbors. Her shoulder blades embraced the tree as she leaned back. The muddy gown clung to her skin and she shivered.

Carlos saw his father emerge from the darkness of the field. He walked past him and entered the barn. Carlos knew not to follow him.

After a few minutes the broad doors of the barn opened and Frank drove the wagon out. He stopped in front of the house and looked down at his son.

"Papa, where's Momma?"

"Get back in the house and mind your sister. I'm gonna take your momma to the doctor. She's sick."

He drove the wagon across the field and down the hill toward the creek.

Cordelia sat on the edge of a chair at the far end of the dogtrot, hugging the handle of the ax to her chest, its head on the floor, the balls of her feet resting where the handle met the blade. That's where Carlos found her.

"Come on, Cordi, Papa said for us to get to sleep."

Later, Carlos sat in the bed, unable to close his eyes. He could survey all the contents of their room in a single glance. The bed, a trunk under the window at the front of the house, and a table with an enamel wash basin and pitcher. The four walls were bare except for the hooks of clothes and the tattered church calendar on the wall at the foot of the bed. He stared at the picture on the calendar. A boy and a girl walked on a rotting wooden bridge across a dark ravine. The girl carried a tiny lamb. An angel in pink and blue robes, surrounded by bright yellow light, floated just behind them.

The angel frightened him. It seemed like a warning to boys like him. The hours spent sitting next to his mother on church pews had taught him how to understand the picture. The angel was there to watch the children, to follow them wherever they went. And when the children were in dangerous places, like the bridge, the angel's job was to push them over the edge or make certain that they stepped into the holes left by the missing treads. But the angel would only do this if the children had sinned. When Carlos heard the preacher use the word retribution, he always imagined the angel.

He knew that the angel would always be with him and his sister. Always just behind them. Always over their shoulders. Watching for sin and an opportunity to punish them.

The doctor and constable stood behind the oak desk as Frank told them his wife's story. She was an Indian from Oklahoma and he had married her out of pity. He told them how she had never been completely right, how she refused to give her twin boys names when they were born and instead let the nuns at the Territory hospital give them those damned Mexican names, Carlos and Pablo. He told them they would not believe how those Indians lived up there. He also told them the story of a dead bloody child, their boy Pablo, and how she refused to bury him for four days, how he had had to force her fingers from around the boy's arms, how she had thrown herself into his grave. He told them how she had never been the same since then. And he told them what she had done that very night. Or tried to do.

While he told her story, Sarah sat locked in a room at the back of the constable's office, wrapped in a green wool blanket. The constable could not bring himself to put a woman in his single cell. Even an Indian woman.

Neither the doctor nor the constable knew this man, but they had to believe his story.

The constable leaned over to motion for the doctor to sign the papers first. The constable then signed and gave the pen to Frank. He held it awkwardly. The doctor nodded toward the constable.

"Mister Dews, you can just make a cross or an X if you want."

Frank followed the constable's finger to its end and made a small X on the paper. The constable took the pen from him and wrote something next to it.

Frank Dews (his mark).

Frank looked down. His dirty hand had left a smudge on the paper.

The constable told Frank that someone from the state would come to get her in a few days. He would make sure she was taken care of until then.

The following days, the women of the town talked about the poor crazy Indian woman brought to the constable's office in the middle of the night. The constable's wife told of the knock on their door and how the woman screamed as the constable and the crazy woman's husband sat in the seat of the wagon riding to the office, the woman tied up in the back, wearing only a cotton-sack shift, thrashing from side to side, begging for help from anyone.

And the men of the town talked of that poor Dews man, working one of the farms out there on the Williams place. They did not know how he was going to make it with two children and no woman to take care of them, keep the house, and cook. They all agreed he should have known better than to marry an Indian.

1908

Cordelia cooked eggs for her brother and Carlos milked the cow and turned the chickens out of their pen. They knew their chores and knew to do them even when their father was not at home. When they heard the jangle of the tack and the heavy plod of the mules' hooves on the packed sand road, Cordelia and Carlos, barefoot and still wearing their night shirts, ran to the front of the house and sat on the top porch step, their arms around their shins and their chins on their knees. They followed the wagon's invisible progress through the woods. When it finally emerged from the tunnel of trees and entered the broad field in front of the house, they jumped to their feet.

He was alone.

The children exchanged a glance. The mules turned from the road and climbed the shallow bank. Their father stopped the wagon in front of the house.

"Your momma's going to the state hospital in some place called Terrell. If she gets all right she'll come on home to us." He continued before the children could respond. "Now Cordi, you get in there and fix me something to eat. Carlos, take the mules in the barn and hitch them to the big disk. Mister Williams thinks we should break that patch down by the creek one more time before we plant it."

That night, after Cordelia was asleep, Carlos and Frank sat at either end of the table in the dogtrot, eating cornbread soaked in buttermilk from tin cups. When he was done, Frank put his cup down on the table and picked up the coal oil lamp. He paused outside the door to his room.

"Son, I don't want you to tell Cordi this, but that ax your momma had last night was for you and your sister. She was gonna hurt you. She said the Lord told her that there was something evil in you and your sister, and that she had to kill you for it. She said it was why Pablo had died too. She said it had come from mixing her blood with my blood. I had to stop her. And she said the preacher told her that the only way to keep the evil away from you was for you to do good works, to work hard and show that you love the Lord by your work."

Carlos stared at the cup on the table in front of him. Frank closed the door to his room behind him.

He never again mentioned their mother. And they would never see her again.

1928

At fourteen Mildred was the oldest of the seven children of David and Florence Scogin, all born within twelve short years. David Weldon was next, now thirteen and almost a man. They all called him Brother, since he shared the name David with his papa. The other children, Fairie, Audrey, Raymond, Wesley, and Beamon, ranged in age from eleven to two.

The six older children had their own cotton sacks and were expected to pick, weed, or chop cotton every day. The seventh child, Beamon, was too young to pick and usually wandered among the rows. He was Mildred's baby in the fields, since their mother was pregnant again, at home and having trouble.

Mildred thought it had been a sign from the Lord that Beamon was to be her momma's last baby, since she had him on the same day they thought that Jesus was coming back. They were all working in the field that day, hoeing a pea patch over on the Lunsford place. They heard it before they saw it, a loud stuttering buzz, like a big bumblebee. When it flew over them, they thought it was the beginning of the end of the world. A big cross flying through the sky to announce Jesus's return. Their momma's water broke the moment she saw it. When PapaDavid went into town the next day, the people in the square told him that it was an airplane and not the Lord.

But Beamon wasn't the last baby. That was two years ago and now their momma was pregnant again. This time they were working the Nalls's cotton fields. Twelve acres of sandy red soil owned by Mister Johnny Nall, three miles down the dusty road from where they lived. The Scogins sharecropped on land owned by Mister Bolin, but their father contracted the family out year round to chop cotton in the spring and pick it in the fall.

Beamon was exhausted and began to fret, distracting Mildred from her picking.

"Beamon, why don't you come over here to my row? You can sit down on the end of my sack and I'll pull you along on it."

With hands and feet caked from the dirt of the field, the boy did as he was asked and sat down on the tail end of Mildred's cotton sack.

Mildred was one of the best cotton pickers in the county. Her nimble fingers and flickering nervousness helped. That and a quick eye. She worked by alternating her hands, pulling the cotton from one bole with one hand while the other pitched its cotton just inside the rim of her sack. Mildred always used the same cotton sack. She could spot it among the pile of sacks in the bed of the wagon by the way she tied the end over with a bow, the same one she used when tying the bow of her Sunday church dress behind her back, the same one she used when tying the shoes of her younger brothers and sisters. Nobody knew how she learned to tie a bow that way and she wouldn't teach anyone else how it was done.

She was small and quick. At church on Sunday or when they sometimes went to town, PapaDavid would tell people to look at how skinny his girl was, what a pretty figure she already had. He'd spin her around, put a hand on each side of her waist and show people how the tips of his thumbs and fingertips could touch.

Mildred pulled Beamon along as she picked, drawing the long sack toward her until it bunched at her feet. She picked until the bag, with her brother's weight pinning it to the ground, was extended to

its full length, three times the length of her body. At first Beamon sat
on the sack, looking back down the row at the smooth trail left behind in the sandy soil. But after only a few minutes, Mildred noticed
him lying on the sack with his heels hanging off the edge, leaving two
narrow traces in the soil behind them. After a few more minutes he
was curled on his side, asleep.

"Girl, stop draggin that boy on your sack. He's slowin you down.
You put him down in the shade under a bush at the side of the field
or under the seat of the wagon. You can hear him if he wakes up
and starts in crying. Your momma in the bed, like she is, already has
us down a pair of hands. And I ain't gonna let you slack off just because you got that baby to look after." Their father always barked at
his children. He never saw a reason to speak to them unless it was to
correct the way they were doing something or to give them an order
to do the next thing.

PapaDavid wouldn't let Mildred stay at home with their mother.
He wanted her to pick her share of the cotton. He was determined
for them to pick at least a bale, a full twelve hundred pounds, each
day. At twenty-five cents per one-hundred pounds, the Scogins, if
they all worked together, could earn three dollars a day.

Mildred liked to keep moving, but the monotony of picking cotton was almost more than she could bear. She set goals for herself
just to stay amused, and sometimes raced Brother to see who could
finish a row first. She always kept an eye on the wagon at the edge
of the fields where they weighed and dumped the cotton when their
sacks were full. Mildred looked forward to these breaks when they
climbed a ladder at the side of the tall wire-slatted wagon bed, mind-
ful that a slip with the strap around their neck could snap it or at
least pull them down to the ground with the force of the heavy sack.
Brother broke his arm when he was ten years old just that way. PapaDavid beat him all the way home then most of the way to the
doctor's office. He had to pick cotton the rest of the season using
just one hand.

Mildred carried Beamon toward the end of the field, took a ragged quilt from the bed of the wagon and spread it on the pine straw

at the edge of the woods. She laid him at its center, shooed away two flies that had settled on his face, and checked the ground to ensure that no ant beds were nearby. She broke off a limb from a sassafras bush and stuck the end of it at an angle into the sandy soil, so the leaves hovered just above his face. She hoped the leaves moving in the breeze would keep the flies off of him. She patted Beamon on his dirty round belly and walked back to her work.

PapaDavid and her brothers and sisters continued making their way down the long rows toward the far end of the field. Their father wouldn't let any of the children pause for a drink of water until they were at the end of a row.

Mildred measured her work by counting the number of times she gathered the sack near to her. After every five adjustments, she stood and cocked her head toward where Beamon slept. She knew he would be scared if he woke up alone at the edge of the woods.

PapaDavid and her brothers and sisters continued making their way down the long rows toward the far end of the field. Her father turned to Brother. "Boy, you sure are making that cotton look awfully raggedy. Pick them boles clean. I don't want Mister Nall docking us for leaving cotton in the field. I'm bound and determined to have him hire us again next year."

Mildred had made smaller cotton sacks from corn meal bags for the younger children. For her father, babies meant hands and hands meant more cotton picked at the end of the day. None of his neighbors started their children working in the fields as early as he did. As soon as they were able to walk at his side and understand his instructions, he brought them to the field. When they got old enough to pick on a row by themselves, their father made Mildred or Brother pick behind the little ones to make sure there wasn't any cotton left behind.

They picked row after row and sack after sack as the shade from the tall pines around the field made its way across the rows of cotton. At least the heat of summer was gone. Mildred's mother always said that it was a sign that the Lord loved them that cotton was not ready for picking in the middle of the summer heat. She said He wouldn't make it both such hard work and ready in the heat of the summer too.

"Mildred, you need to quit pickin a bit early so you can get back to the house to start fixin some dinner and see if your momma needs anything. Take the little ones with you. When they get this tired they are almost more trouble than they're worth. Me and your brothers will finish up these last rows and be back home about dark. Now you have us some supper ready when we get home, you hear?"

Mildred walked back to where Beamon lay in the edge of the woods. He was still in the center of the quilt, a stream of saliva bridging his lip to the cloth.

"Come on, Beamon, wake up baby, we going home."

On the walk home they passed the houses of some of the children who had gone to school with Mildred at the Redland one-room schoolhouse. The families sat on their porches and waved as the Scogin children walked by. Mildred didn't know these children very well because her papa made her quit school after fifth grade when her momma had trouble having Beamon. Mildred had to help with the babies and work around the house. And as her papa always said, Mildred had learned how to read and write and do some figures so she didn't need any more schooling.

Mildred's only chance of escape from her father was through marriage. And although she was only fourteen, she already had her eyes open for possible husbands, mostly boys her own age or a little older that she remembered from school or saw at church. The one thing Mildred knew for sure was that she wanted to find a husband as soon as possible and that she wanted her husband to be different from her papa. She made herself pretty when they went to church on Sundays and whenever she thought she might see any young men.

They crossed the creek at the Lunsford place and made their way through the pine woods to the Fitzy junction, where the road ran south to Nacogdoches and north, eventually to Texarkana. The road they were on ran east to Louisiana, just one county away, and the road to the west road ran endlessly across the rest of Texas. They crossed the busy Nacogdoches road then climbed the last hill home.

When they walked in their own yard, they went directly to the well where Mildred drew a bucket of cold water. They drank from the tin dipper, youngest to oldest. Mildred went inside. Their momma was asleep on the bed.

Mildred walked back out onto the porch. "Yawl run on out and play or just sit on up here on the porch and rest. Momma's sleepin and we don't need to wake her up. Just stay right around here and be good."

She fed the chickens and began to chop the wood for the stove to cook dinner. She heard the screen door on the back porch slam and looked up to see Beamon walking toward her, his hands and arms stained with something dark.

"Beamon, come here, baby. What have you got all over your little hands? You better not have been in them preserves. Come here, let Sister see."

Mildred walked to the edge of the porch where Beamon stood, grabbed his arms and pulled him to her.

"Are you hurt, baby? Let me see. Where did that blood come from?"

Mildred checked his arms and hands but found no source for the blood. She ran inside the house, leaving Beamon whimpering on the porch. She looked in the kitchen and the boys' room. She ran down the center hall of the house onto the front porch, thinking the dogs had killed a chicken. But the porch was clean. She ran into the room where the boys slept but found nothing there. The girls kept their door latched so he couldn't have been in there. She saw the door to her parents' room open. She looked inside. Her mother was still sleeping soundly.

On the floor next to the bed Mildred saw a smear of blood extending from under the edge of the bed, ending with a pair of small handprints. She walked to the side of the bed, dropped to her knees, and looked under the bed. From the sag of the feather mattress supporting her mother's body Mildred saw a drop of blood fall into a puddle on the floor beneath it. She jumped to her feet and shook her mother.

"Oh Momma, wake up, wake up."

Her mother didn't move.

Mildred threw back the thin quilt and sheet. Her mother's night-gown was pulled up around her waist. One of her mother's legs was bent at the knee, the toes curled under. The other leg was perfectly straight, toes pointed toward the end of the bed. A crimson pool had formed in the mattress around her mother's butt. Slowly moving in the blood, as if trying to swim, was a tiny baby, still attached to its mother by a dirty gray cord.

Mildred put her hand over her mother's mouth and nose. She didn't feel any breath. She buried her face against her mother's neck. Her mother's skin was cool and she sagged in Mildred's arms. Her head doddled as Mildred shook with sobs.

"Oh Momma. Momma. Please wake up. We need you, Momma. We can't get by without you."

The baby below made a kacking sound, a mixture of liquid and air, as it struggled in the pond of shit and blood.

With one hand cradling her neck, Mildred stared into her mother's blank face and traced the length of her mother's body with her hand. Her fingers passed the edge of her gown and once again touched cold flesh. The baby's skin was only slightly warmer when her fingers found it. Mildred couldn't bring herself to look at it again. She closed her eyes. Her fingers followed the shape of the baby's body to the crown of its head. She then found its narrow neck. Mildred knew that what she was doing was best. Best for it. Best for everyone.

She encircled its tiny throat with her thumb and index finger and held tight. She opened her eyes and stared at her mother's face and waited for the baby to join its mother.

Mildred pulled the cover back over them, closed the door and walked to the porch. She called to her brother resting under the shade of the chinaberry tree at the side of the house.

"Wesley, run back to the field and get Daddy and Brother. Tell them they gotta come home right now. Momma's real sick."

Mildred walked down the porch steps and to the well to draw another bucket of water.

1929

Mildred had heard about the Dews boy who lived on the Williams place outside Garrison. She heard what people said about him, and the rumors about why Mister Williams kept him on the place, but she couldn't believe it. People were just jealous. He worked hard and Mister Williams treated him like a son. They said that Dews boy was the hardest working man in the county.

The only problem people saw in him was that he wouldn't take up with a woman no matter how much any woman had tried. He had been with plenty of women, he just wouldn't choose one in particular. And the girls Mildred knew who had met him said he was handsome, tall, with the bluest eyes anyone had seen, even though his mother was an Indian from Oklahoma. They said that blue eyes in the Dews men must be strong to win out over Indian brown eyes. They said his daddy, that mean old Dews man who still lived out there in the woods back of the Williams place, the one who hated niggers so much and worked like a dog every day, had the same blue eyes and was as mean as a snake. Mildred knew that his name was Carlos, but that he wasn't Mexican, and that he was at least ten years older than she was. She was fifteen and he was more than twenty-five.

This was all she knew of him, besides the rumors, when Mary Alice Hart asked her after church if she wanted to walk all the way up to the Fitzy Hill that evening to meet the Lunsford boy she was sweet on. Mary Alice said that the Dews boy would be with him because they were going coon hunting as soon as it got dark, and that Lee wanted her to bring a friend to keep Carlos busy while she and Lee went walking around in the woods. Mildred and Mary Alice both knew what walking around in the woods really meant.

Mary Alice walked back home with Mildred and her family after church and had Sunday dinner with them. She helped Mildred kill a couple of hens, gut, skin, batter, and fry them. Mildred had made collards the night before that were waiting in the cast iron pot on the stove. The girls washed some potatoes and made flour and dootchie gravy in the chicken grease. After dinner, with all the children scattered through the house and yard, napping or playing, Mildred and Mary Alice slipped out the back door for their long walk. On a Sunday evening, PapaDavid didn't mind if she disappeared for a few hours with one of her friends, as long as all the kids had been fed and would stay out of his hair as he wrote his weekly neighborhood column for the Nacogdoches newspaper. But he sure didn't want her to find someone to marry and take her away, at least until Beamon was old enough to take care of himself.

"Mary Alice, what do you know about him? I don't like that name Carlos."

"You know as much about him as I do. You'll have to ask him yourself. It'll give you something to talk about. All I know is that he and his sister were raised without their momma. His little sister took care of their daddy and Carlos after that, until she married one of the Skeltons and left them. And this Carlos has lived almost his whole life on the Williams place. He lives in that little white house right behind the big Williams house. You must have seen it."

They were to meet a half mile off the main Nacogdoches road down an old logging trail, in a clearing where lightning had struck a huge pine tree many years before. The tree had rotted and fallen bit by bit with only the rich heart of stump left standing in the center of the clearing. It was cold, and Mildred and Mary Alice walked next to one another with arms linked and shoulders hunched, their cloth coats and thin cotton socks not warm enough against the chill of the damp December afternoon.

As they neared the clearing, a blue tick hound ran out of the bushes toward them. Mary Alice squealed and Mildred lifted her foot to kick the dog to the side. "Lee, if you're out there you better come get this dog. Mildred will kick it to death." Both girls laughed.

Smiling, Lee Lunsford and another man walked out of the thick pine saplings at the edge of the clearing. Mildred was surprised at just how good-looking the stranger was. But she thought he would look even better and taller still if he didn't stoop and look down at the ground the way he did. Both men wore quilted denim coats and the other man carried a double-barreled shotgun over his shoulder. He whistled and the dog ran to his side. He bent down and scratched it between its ears.

"That dog ain't gonna hurt nobody."

Mildred stood by herself as Mary Alice walked to Lee's side. He opened his coat and folded Mary Alice into it.

"Hey Lee. How ya doin?"

"I'm just fine, Mildred, and you?"

"I'm fine, Lee."

"Carlos, this is my gal Mary Alice Hart and this is her friend Mildred Scogin."

"Howdy." Carlos nodded.

Mary Alice looked up at Lee and then to Mildred. "Me and Lee's gonna walk around in the woods to keep warm. Yawl fine just staying here and talking?"

Mildred looked up at Carlos. "I guess so."

Carlos looked at Lee. "Unless that dog trails a coon, then I'm gonna follow it."

Lee and Mary Alice disappeared into the thicket of pine and hardwood scrub. Mildred shivered and crossed her arms across her chest.

"You want me to light a fire? I could break off some of that heart pine and make a hot fire real quick."

"Yes, that would be mighty nice, Carlos. Thank you."

Carlos began breaking pieces of heartwood from the hard, high stump in the center of the clearing. He seemed to welcome the chance to have something to do, to keep him moving and busy. Mildred stomped her feet and put her hands inside her coat as she watched him work.

"I don't know why nobody hasn't come to get this heart pine for kindling before. It's as rich as can be and right here just off the road. Either it's too far for them to haul or they just don't know it's here. If I had a wagon of my own I would have done got it a long time ago. Here, smell this."

Carlos gave Mildred a small piece of the wood. She took it and inhaled the sweet smell of the heavy amber heartwood.

Carlos made a stack of the rich kindling near the edge of the clearing and started the fire with a silver lighter he took from the breast pocket of his overalls. Mildred walked up to the fire as soon as it caught. Carlos walked to her side. "I'll go drag up some big pieces once it gets going good."

"Thank you. This fire sure feels good. I was fixin to freeze to death." Mildred warmed her hands, then turned her back to the fire. "Carlos, I like your name. But where does it come from? You the first Carlos I've ever met, or even heard of, except for Mexicans, and you don't look like no Mexican to me."

"Well, I ain't no damned Mexican, that's for sure. I got this name from my momma. Or it was at least because of her that I got it."

"I heard your momma was an Indian."

"Yeah, she was an Indian and that's part of the story."

Carlos moved to the other side of the fire, opposite Mildred, and squatted. He looked into the fire as it grew.

"She come from up in Oklahoma somewhere. Back before it was even a state. Indian Territory still when I was born up there. I was a twin, had a twin brother named Pablo—another Mexican name—but he died when we was little. When we was born, at least this is how Daddy tells the story, our momma wanted to have us at home like everybody else did there, with her momma helping her, but Daddy didn't want no Indian woman helping bring his babies into the world, so he made our momma go to a hospital on the reservation run by some of them Catholic nuns. Well, that made her so mad that she didn't want to have anything to do with us at first. Daddy said he should have known there was something wrong with her right then. According to Daddy she wouldn't have anything to do with us, not even hold us or look at us or anything—Daddy said it was like when you mess with a baby bird in a nest, how you leave your scent on it and the momma bird will stop feeding it and let it die. It was that way with us. They had to start us out on cow's milk since our momma wouldn't even let us suck. When it came time for us to leave the hospital one of the nurses said that they had to have names for the babies and our momma wouldn't give us no names, not even some Indian name, wouldn't say a word when Daddy asked her, so Daddy told the nurse to give us names. Said he would change em later if he didn't like em. Said a man couldn't come up with no names, that that was for a woman to do."

Carlos's coon dog trotted back into the clearing and curled up next to him. He reached down and pulled softly on one of its long ears.

"So this one nun was a Mexican and said her brothers' names was Carlos and Pablo, so Daddy said for her to use those names. Just to spite Momma. So that's how come I'm Carlos. My little sister said Momma wanted to change our names later on but Daddy wouldn't let her or it cost too much to do it or something."

Mildred looked across the fire at Carlos's face. He was staring at the ground in front of him. "So she did take up with you then, sometime."

"Yeah, after a few days Daddy said her titties were swelled up so big and hurting that she didn't have no choice but to let us suck on her. And that's all it took for her to get over it."

"And what happened to your momma? She don't live with your daddy, does she? She still alive?"

"No, she . . ."

He choked on the words. A single tear ran down his cheek. He swallowed hard.

"No, she died up in Terrell a few years back. She done something bad when we was little so she was over in Terrell. You know what I mean?"

"Yeah. You mean the state hospital? But what was wrong with her?"

"She lost her mind. You know when I told you that my little brother died? Well that was the beginning of it. But Daddy says he should have seen it coming earlier. After Pablo got killed she sort of lost her mind, and Daddy had to have her committed. That was when I was about ten."

Carlos picked at the fire with a twig. Mildred walked around the fire and squatted next to him.

"My momma died just last year. Trying to have another baby. I got six brothers and sisters and I'm pretty much their momma now. The baby died too." Mildred turned to look at Carlos. He glanced at her, then shook his head and stared back at the fire. "You get along with your daddy?"

"Yeah, I guess so. But I work for Mister Williams now. Daddy still works on the place but I don't have that much to do with him. How about you and your daddy?"

"You've probably heard about my daddy. He works us awfully hard. All of us. He's especially hard on my brother Weldon and me, since we're the oldest. With Momma gone he expects me to do all her work and to help raise the little ones. I don't know what he will do when I get married and move off on my own."

"My daddy was the same way too. Worked us hard. My sister got married as soon as she could. Then I started working for Mister Williams. Daddy's been on his own since then." Carlos stood and turned his back to the fire. He offered Mildred a hand and she stood up next to him. "You and that Hart girl walk over here from her daddy's place?"

"No, we walked from my daddy's place over at Redland."

"You two done walked all that way and expecting to walk back before it gets dark on you?"

"Yeah, and if Mary Alice and Lee don't get back soon it will be long past dark when we get home."

Carlos looked into the woods in the direction where Lee and Mary Alice had disappeared. He whistled the call of a whippoorwill. He cocked his head to the side. Lee answered with the same call.

"They over that ridge up toward the Key place. You want me to walk you back home?"

Mildred looked up at Carlos. "You mean walk the way they are doing or just walk me straight home?"

"Walk you directly back home."

"Well, that's mighty nice, but won't that be an awful lot of walking for you, and didn't you want to do some coon hunting tonight with Lee?"

"Shoot no. That's not far. I can walk from Nacogdoches back to the Williams place just this side of Garrison during the night then plow a full day the next day, if I have to. And if Blue trees a coon on the way back home from Redland then I'll do some hunting too."

Carlos turned back in the direction of Lee's call and made a sound that was a cross between the way Mildred's daddy called his cattle up to the barn and the way the old veterans of the Civil War yelled in their parades that they called a rebel yell.

"That's the signal Lee and me have that we use when we are deer hunting. It means that we haven't seen no sign of any deer and that I'm heading home my way and he can do the same on his end. Listen, if he hollers back at us in just a minute it means he is fine with that. I bet he's asking Mary Alice if it's okay."

Lee echoed Carlos's yelp.

"And I reckon that means he will walk the Hart girl home himself, especially since it's a lot closer than our walk."

They turned from the fire and walked back toward the main road.

Carlos walked Mildred to within sight of her daddy's house. It had been dark for almost an hour when the Scogin house came into view. Mildred had warned Carlos about PapaDavid and how she wasn't supposed to be seeing any boys. And how she and Mary Alice had lied about where they were going that night.

They stood facing one another, at the edge of the woods near her father's house.

"Well, little lady, I sure have enjoyed talking and walking with you tonight."

"Me too, Carlos."

"And I've been seeing one of Lee's cousins, Clara Little, over by Cold Springs, but we just stopped courting, and I sure wouldn't mind seeing you again sometime soon."

"I'd like that too. Maybe the next time Lee and Mary Alice plan to meet we could too. Just like they was doing tonight."

"I'd sure appreciate that. Now, you gonna be fine walking the rest of the way by yourself?"

"I'll be fine. Even if a mad dog got after me here, I could outrun it to the porch."

"Well, I'll see you then."

Carlos turned to walk away as Mildred took her first step toward home. Carlos reached over and touched her shoulder as she stepped away. She stopped and they looked at one another. Mildred would always remember this. It was the first time they ever touched.

In the one-hundred steps it took her to reach the front porch of her father's house, Mildred decided that she would marry Carlos Dews. She decided that this man, who had a funny name, a crazy momma, a dead twin brother, and a mean daddy of his own, could take her away from PapaDavid. In exchange for saving her from the double duty of sister and momma to all those little ones and taking her away from a mean daddy, she could figure out exactly what this man needed and give it to him. No matter what it was.

She could see a deep hurt in his eyes and she wanted to be a balm to that hurt. Just like a momma doesn't decide which of the things she's gonna give her baby, she would give him everything he needed and he would grow and grow. And she could heal the cause of his pain. And that stooping back of his would straighten with pride. Pride she would give him. And he would be grateful and proud, and would love her for it.

The next morning, as she woke then fed the children, cleaned the house and got ready to do laundry, Mildred couldn't stop thinking about Carlos. She knew she loved him already, and that he would love her too. Everybody always called him the Dews boy over on the Williams place, but she knew he was a man, and that he was going to be her man too.

As she stood filling the sink with a kettle of hot water, PapaDavid walked in from meeting the mailman down at the road. He entered with a smile on his face that Mildred knew meant the mailman had passed on a good piece of gossip or genuine news from the wider world.

"I guess folks will have some excitement to talk about for the next few days."

"What do you mean, PapaDavid?"

"Well, I just was talking with Johnny and he said that somebody just about caught the world afire last night."

"What do you mean?"

"He said that somebody started a fire in them fine pine woods over next to the Key place, on the Fitzy Hill, and it got out and must have burned at least four hundred acres of good pine timberland. Said that half the county turned out to try to stop it from spreading. Folks hitched their mules and plowed fire rows to keep it from spreading. Even plowed with lanterns in the middle of the night. Johnny said he was surprised we hadn't noticed the glow in the sky from it or even smelled it burning. Said most of the county could see or smell it, but that the wind must not have been in our direction last night. He said Mister Key was as mad as he ever seen him when he came into town this morning. Said he would prosecute if he ever found out who started that fire."

Mildred continued to wash the dishes in the scalding water and repeat to herself, just about caught the world afire, just about caught the world afire, just about caught the world afire. She was certain it was a sign from the Lord.

1930

Mildred sat next to Carlos on the seat of the rubber-tired wagon as they drove to the county seat to be married. Mister Williams had a friend with a house just outside of Nacogdoches who
only used it on the weekends, when he and his family went into town
to do his buying for the farm. He was more than happy to offer it to
Carlos and Mildred for their wedding night. They would spend their
first night there, across the road from the big new cemetery where
the rich people of Nacogdoches were to be buried. Mildred had only
been to Nacogdoches a few times during her life, and Carlos had to
explain to her where the house was so she could imagine it and think
about where they were going to spend their honeymoon.

Carlos told her that they had arrived at the edge of town when
the old red brick silo came into sight as they topped the hill at the
road that turned off to the Old North Church. But they weren't going to be married in a church. Her father wouldn't pay for a wedding
he didn't approve of, and Carlos said he didn't trust no preacher to
do nothing except bury the dead. Carlos liked to go to the harp singing at the Brileytown Church, but that was just for the singing. He
didn't know how to read and didn't trust anything that a preacher
read from a book, even when they tried to turn the words on the

page into something that they thought he might understand. No. He didn't trust any of them. He told Mildred of too many times hearing preachers yelling out from the pulpits about the sins of drink and fornication, when he knew well what the preacher men were doing as soon as they got away from town, or out in the woods somewhere with a group of other men. He knew how they talked when they weren't near women or standing in the front of the church.

So there was no church wedding for them. Just the Justice of the Peace at the Nacogdoches courthouse, with a ring that Carlos bought from a man who took it off his wife's finger before he kicked her out of his house and sent her back to her parents. But Mildred wouldn't know that, like so many other things, until years had passed.

It was hot, so Mildred wore one of her lightest dresses, a cream-colored Sunday dress she and her sister Audrey had made special the night before by sewing on some lace they found in a box of notions their dead momma had left in the trunk in the hallway. Nobody would know it was her wedding dress unless she told them, even with the new lace at the collar, around the sleeves, and at the waist.

Mildred had known the ride down to Nacogdoches would take almost half the day, so she wore a broad-brimmed straw hat and brought a switch her daddy had made out of a horse's tail to keep the biting flies off of her when they drove through the bottom lands and over the creeks.

They stood in front of the JP's desk, Mildred's head level with Carlos's chest, as they repeated the old man's words. Carlos looked down at the floor and Mildred looked over at the justice's secretary, their witness, who sat in a straight-backed chair next to the JP's desk. Carlos kept his broad hand in the small of Mildred's back, some-times pushing against her back so hard, like he was having to keep her there. She had to lean back against his hand to keep her balance and not take a step forward. She couldn't help but feel dirty, like they were doing something they weren't supposed to do. She felt that the JP and his clerk were going to talk nasty about them as soon as they walked out of the office door, talk about this too young girl marrying this too old man.

But Mildred liked the feeling of the two of them together. She had spent her entire life living as a bunch. That Scogin bunch. "That Scogin bunch over at Redland," people would say. On her wedding night, after she and Carlos were done and they had both collapsed down next to each other on the bed and she had heard him breathing to sleep, she couldn't help but think that this was what the words the JP said had meant. That there was something magic in his words and that they were two become one, just like when the preacher dunked her under the water and she had come up out of that water different from when she had walked down the creek bank only a few minutes before. They were one, just the two of them. And they would stay that way, forever. She was sure that what he had just done would be enough. No matter what else happened, if they had this, it would be enough to keep them together. She didn't know where it came from, but she kept thinking of the words "the ties that bind." The ties that bind.

Mildred hadn't ever spent the night in a bed with a man, but she knew pretty much what they did there. She was only sixteen but had seen enough cows and horses and goats and chickens to know what was involved. The only difference she knew of was the kissing part, and she and Carlos had already done that too, on their walks in the woods. And her daddy's sister, Aunt Neva, had told her just the day before about the pain and bleeding that would probably happen.

Carlos was much older and she knew he had already been with other women. He would know what to do.

And he did. When he came back into the bedroom that night, after she asked him to step out a minute to let her put her night clothes on and get into the bed, Mildred noticed something different about him. He walked back into the bedroom carrying his shoes, the laces tied together and hanging from the first two fingers of his right hand. He was still wearing the same shirt and dark blue overalls, new, that he had worn all day. Mildred noticed that his shirt collar was unbuttoned and that the skin of his face and neck was red from a good soap scrubbing. He reminded her of her little brothers and sisters when she checked to make sure they had washed their faces and behind their ears each night before putting them to bed. She was sad, thinking that this was the first night in her siblings' lives that they would be put to bed by someone other than her or their mother.

Carlos walked to the opposite side of the bed and hung his shoes from the back of a ladderback chair. As he unsnapped the two shoulder buckles of his overalls and tossed the strap back over his shoulders, and dropped the overalls to the floor, Mildred saw something in Carlos she had never seen before. In public places he often kept his chin tucked and his eyes toward the ground, his stooped shoulders folding inward and down. But standing here, by the side of their marriage bed, he seemed at least a foot taller, assured of himself. He seemed suddenly certain that he controlled everything within the realm of the room. He appeared confident that no one was his better here.

He turned to face the bed, wearing only his unbuttoned shirt, the tails hanging open and to his thighs. He unbuttoned the cuffs, lifted the shirt over his shoulders and let it fall to join the overalls on the floor at his feet.

Neither he nor Mildred spoke.

Mildred let her eyes move down from the stark lines where the dark skin of his arms met the white skin protected by his clothes. As her eyes came to his groin, she saw him look at her face. He saw where she was looking. He reached down with his right hand and encircled his balls and the shaft of his penis. He lifted and shook the heavy fist of flesh at her. He smiled.

Mildred looked away and Carlos turned, sat on the edge of the bed, then climbed between the stark white sheets that covered her.

It did hurt some, at first. But beyond the pleasure that came from his weight on her and how tightly they held to one another as they fucked—and she now felt that this was the right word for it, although she had only spoken it aloud once or twice before that night—the thing that impressed and frightened Mildred the most about that night was the change it brought about in Carlos.

She had been drawn to him because she thought he needed her.

She felt she could help him and that he needed her help. He always seemed ashamed about something or that he was always hurting in some kind of deep terrible way. She thought maybe he needed a mother and a sister and that she could be both for him, that she could help him face the world since it seemed he was afraid of something or ashamed of himself. Some people even said he was mean like his daddy, but that wasn't what Mildred saw.

When he walked in with those shoes hanging from his fingers and flicked those overall buckles and dropped that shirt and then lifted and shook those heavy things between his legs, she saw him transformed. He was a man. And when he flicked the top of the sheet that covered them both, lifting it up and making the air and space under the sheet so he could get up on top of her for the first time, she knew he was proud. Proud of what he could do in a bed. Proud that nobody could tell him how to do that any better. Proud that nobody with a book with words or any other school learning had anything to say to him about it. Proud that he knew how to do something naturally, without having to think about it or about anybody outside that room. She could tell that he knew what he was doing, knew that he was doing it right and well. And she was certain he knew that she loved what he was doing, and was going to keep doing to her, and that because of it she would never think of leaving him.

After they had finished, Mildred lay with her head on Carlos's chest, her shoulder tucked under his arm. He kissed the top of her head.

He shifted to reach for the silver alarm clock on the table beside the bed. He picked it up, turned the small knob on its back, and released the lever between the two large bells.

"Why, Carlos, what are you doing with that clock? It's our wedding night. We don't need no alarm in the morning."

"Sugar, I just set it for 4:30 in the morning. I told Mister Williams we would be back on the place before the middle of the day to do some plowing. I told him I'd do some work tomorrow afternoon and that you could hoe that pea patch back behind the house."

"Oh. I just thought that we might have a couple of days together before you had to get back to work for Mister Williams."

"Well, that ain't the way it's gonna be. Mister Williams depends on me. Now that there's two of us he can expect even more work from us. Goodnight, Sugar."

He turned over and was asleep within a few minutes.

Mildred spent the night looking at the wall next to the bed and thinking about her father and her new husband.

1932

Mildred knew he wasn't where he said he would be. After two years of marriage and life on the Williams place, she knew him better than that. But she knew what she had been getting into. Or at least she should have. She had heard what people said about him. Now he had slipped off again and Mildred couldn't find him. But she had an idea and if she was right and it was that widow Effie again then that would be it. She wouldn't put up with it again.

Mildred first checked where he said he would be—in the tool house working on the seeder that damned Schwartz boy broke the day before while planting corn—then went down to the place she imagined he would say he was if she told him she couldn't find him in the tool house. He was not there either. The lot where Mister Williams kept his stud horse waiting for the mares in heat was also empty, so he couldn't use that as his excuse for disappearing from the house for so long on a Sunday afternoon.

She sure didn't want to walk all the way across the creek bottom over to where Effie lived, because she didn't want people to think she was crazy. And she didn't have any business being over there in case he wasn't there and somebody saw her. But they wouldn't do anything over there with all of Effie's children around.

As Mildred turned the corner by the back of the Williams house, she caught a glimpse of blue cloth disappear into the woods across the field. She recognized the color of Carlos's overalls and knew he didn't have any reason to be going into the woods over there. That was the stand of trees that Mister Williams was saving to use to build a house when his daughter got married. There wasn't any stock penned over there that Carlos might have to care for, and she had never seen Carlos walk into those woods before.

She went back into the house and changed her shoes. She put on her work boots and got her momma's old parasol out of the chiffarobe in the bedroom. Walking along the edge of the newly planted cornfield, Mildred made her way to the spot where she saw Carlos disappear.

The years of pine needles falling from the big trees made a carpet that cushioned Mildred's steps as she walked into the dark woods. She folded the parasol and watched her feet to make sure she didn't step on a stray branch. She thought of all the times she and her brothers and sister played hide and seek in the woods on Sunday afternoons, careful just like this. Sometimes they would bend down a sapling to play hobby horse. Or sometimes, if Brother came with them and brought an ax, they would make a flying jinny and spin the kids until they were dizzy.

The tall pine trees were so broad and dense she could only see a few yards in front of her. She walked a zigzag, bending her head and leaning from side to side to see if she could spot them. She looked up at the tops of the trees and saw a place in the distance where they seemed to thin and let in more light. As she got closer, she could see Carlos and Effie standing in the center of the clearing, facing each other, a single step between them.

Mildred wasn't certain what to do next. With a mixture of humiliation and anger, she kept walking toward the clearing, hiding behind a different tree with each few steps. When she got to the edge of the clearing, close enough to hear the sounds they made and to watch the shadows they made on the ground, Mildred couldn't go any farther. She stood and watched, biting into her bottom lip as she saw Carlos drop to his knees in front of Effie and bury his face in the flesh of her stomach. He seemed to breathe through her body, like a crying baby sobs in its mother's lap. He reached under Effie's thin cotton dress, made from a corn meal sack, and pulled down her drawers. He stuffed them into the front pocket of his overalls. He lifted Effie into his arms, then lowered her to the ground. Mildred watched as he took off his overalls but left on his shirt then lowered himself onto her. Mildred wondered how many times they had done this very thing in this very place. She concentrated on the image of him slowly lowering Effie to the ground. One arm around her back and the other up the back of her dress, his hand on her bare backside, lowering her, lowering her, like putting a baby down on a bed. He rested her on the mattress of soft pine straw. Mildred marveled at just how tender he could appear. She knew she should stop them, rush into the clearing. But she couldn't. She wanted to watch them, to confirm what she had been told and long suspected herself. She forced herself to look at what they were doing. She lowered herself, quietly, to the ground at the base of a large pine at the edge of the clearing and watched.

As she saw the white of Carlos's ass clench and his knees dig into the pine straw, Mildred remembered the time that she had watched over his shoulder and into the mirror on the chiffarobe in their bedroom as Carlos was on top of her.

They had tried to warn her about him. They told her why Mister Williams kept him on the place and why Mister Williams liked to keep widow women and their children to work his land. But she couldn't believe them. Would a man take that kind of work? Would he accept that kind of responsibility? Wouldn't he feel some shame? How could he want to be with all those women? How could it work? Wouldn't they be jealous of one another? She remembered the very words that one friend had whispered about Carlos, that he was supposed to keep the women on the place quiet and satisfied. Quiet and satisfied and there. They said it was hard for Mister Williams to get along with most men and he thought that single or widowed women with children appreciated the work and worked harder than married or single men. They said Carlos was different, like a son to Mister Williams. He was raised on the place.

With a soft groan Carlos collapsed onto his elbows on top of Effie. He was done. He stood up and stepped into his overalls. He took her underwear from his pocket and leaned over to help Effie to her feet. The spell was broken for Mildred when she saw Carlos spin Effie around by her shoulder and begin to brush the pine straw from the back of her dress. Seeing him brush the straw was worse than anything else she had witnessed.

Mildred jumped to her feet and stomped into the sunlight of the clearing. "Stop it!" She didn't want to shove Effie or hit Carlos. She just wanted him to stop brushing the pine needles from Effie's back. "No!"

Mildred ran toward them. Carlos stepped between the two women. Mildred threw the parasol at his feet.

"I knew it. Don't even try to lie to me. I been watching the whole time. I should have believed them. I didn't, but I should have. I thought maybe you had changed. Or that what you said was the truth."

Carlos spun around to face Effie. "Get on out of here. Get back to your house. I'll take care of her."

Carlos threw Effie her cotton drawers as if they were on fire. Effie walked backwards to the edge of the clearing, her eyes moving back and forth between Carlos and Mildred, then turned and ran into the thicket of the woods.

Mildred dropped to her knees. She pounded the balls of her hands into the cushion of the forest floor. She gathered two fists of pine straw in her hands.

"Maybe you can't change. It's this damned place. You can only be one way on this place. It's this place."

Mildred gave Carlos a choice that day. They would leave the Williams place as soon as the crops was done that fall or she would leave him and return to her daddy's house.

Carlos gave up what he had on the Williams place for her. It broke his heart to leave the place where he had grown up and she knew it. And although it was his fault they had to leave, she felt she owed him something for having done so. He would never let her forget this, that she had forced him to choose between her and the place where he had lost his mother, the only place he felt he could call home.

1933

Carlos and Mildred moved to the Langston place, three miles south of Garrison on the road to Nacogdoches. Mister Langston was quick to hire Carlos as a hand when he heard Carlos was leaving Mister Williams. Everyone knew that Carlos was the strongest and hardest working man in the county.

They lived just down the hill from the big Langston house, in a small cabin built many years before for Missus Langston's retarded brother. He had drowned in the stock pond a few years back and the house had sat vacant until Carlos and Mildred moved in.

Mister Langston advanced Carlos some of his portion of the next year's crops so he and Mildred could make some improvements to the house. They bought a new wood stove and some rolls of linoleum to keep out the drafts from between the rough floorboards. They used coal oil lamps for light and used the hand pump on the back porch to draw their water. Carlos wouldn't let Mildred spend any of the money on wallpaper to keep out the wind or heavy curtains to cover the windows. He said that it would be a waste of money and they were tough enough to stand a little cold.

On a cool spring morning, a few months after they moved into the little cabin, they sat looking at one another across the wood stove.

There was a knock on the door. Carlos opened it to find the oldest Williams boy standing on their front porch. He looked past Carlos to Mildred at the stove.

"Howdy, Mildred, how you getting along?"

"I'm fine, Bobby. How is your momma?"

"She's just fine, thank you. I'll tell her you asked about her."

"I'd sure appreciate it."

His eyes returned to Carlos. "Can you step out here for a minute, Carlos?"

Carlos closed the door behind him as he stepped onto the porch. He returned in less than a minute. "I need to ride back over to the Williams place with Bobby. And I don't know how long I'll be."

Mildred stood and walked toward the men. "What's wrong? Is Mister Williams sick or hurt or something?"

"No, it's something else."

"What is it?" Mildred looked at Carlos and lowered her voice. "I told you I didn't want you to go back there again."

"Mildred, I have to go." Carlos walked back to the stove and took his coat from the back of his chair.

"What is it, Carlos? Tell me."

"It's Effie. She's having a baby and having trouble with it. She's crying for me and I need to go see her."

"What?"

"Mildred, you have to let me do this."

Carlos walked out the door and slammed it behind him.

Mildred cleaned off the table and washed the dishes, listening into the night for any sign that Carlos was coming back. With the hot water left in the belly of the stove, she filled a dish pan and washed herself for bed. She put on her gown.

Most days Mildred went right to sleep, exhausted from her day's work, but she couldn't keep her eyes closed. She convinced herself that the sound of the wind in the bushes outside the bedroom window was Bobby Williams's truck bringing Carlos back, or that the dogs barking up at the big house meant that Carlos was walking up the lane from the main road.

She sat on top of the bedcovers and stared at the oval wood frame at the foot of the bed, a photograph of her when she was only one year old. It must have been about the time that Brother was born. She wore a frilly white dress and a bonnet trimmed with lace. Mildred once asked her mother about the circumstances of the photograph, since she couldn't remember when it was made and she never knew such a nice dress or bonnet, not even in the clothes handed down to her brothers and sisters. Her mother told her that the photograph was made on her first birthday, that the dress and bonnet belonged to the photographer, and that she had had the hardest time keeping Mildred still enough for the man to make the picture. Her daddy insisted that they take their little girl to town on her first birthday, since they had had three babies before her and not a one had lived 365 days and he wanted a picture of her on that day.

Mildred woke to sunlight streaming through the window beside the bed. She knew she hadn't slept that late since they lived in this cabin because she had never felt the sun shining on the bed with her in it. She wondered what time it was, but knew that Carlos had his watch in his pocket and they didn't have another clock in the house.

She began her regular day's work. She went to the outhouse, let the chickens out of their coop, washed up, got dressed, built a fire in the stove, and started a pot of coffee. She wasn't sure what to do when she finished her morning housework, since Carlos always had a list of things for her to do each day. After cleaning the house, making the bed, warming then eating day-old biscuits with cream gravy, washing her dishes, and putting them away in the pie safe, Mildred looked around for something else to do to occupy her mind. There was nothing.

She walked onto the front porch, took the saddle blanket hanging over the porch rail, folded it, and put it on top of an old milk can next to the front door. She leaned back against the wall of the cabin and realized that it was the first time since they had left the Williams place that she had had time to sit on the front porch. She was surprised to notice her breath, to sense that she did breathe in and out every few seconds, even when she wasn't aware of the air going in and out.

What was she to do? Was that baby his? It must have been, or Effie wouldn't have called for him. How many more were there over on the Williams place? And could he ever change his ways? Could a man who had lived that way that long change his ways? She had threatened to go back to her family, but she had promised herself that she would die before living under the same roof with PapaDavid again.

She would just have to love Carlos through it. Love him so much that he would change. She was sure she could make him change. Love him no matter what he put her through because when they came out of it together, on the other side, he would realize what she had done and why she had done it and love her, just her. What else could she do?

She heard the truck when it changed gears and slowed to make the turn from the highway onto the dirt road. Looking up toward the big house, she saw the dogs begin to stir and stand and stretch from their broadside spots in the sun. They heard it too. Maybe it wasn't him. It could be one of the people who lived down their road coming back from town. But she recognized Bobby's pickup when he turned off the lane and into the circle driveway beside the main house up the hill.

Carlos sat in the passenger's seat, his arm on the edge of the open window, his forehead resting on his arm. She could only see the top of his head, but she recognized him. The truck stopped and Carlos stepped out. His face was bright red and he stooped as if he had been plowing behind a mule for two days without rest. Mildred remained on the milk can as Carlos walked down the hill toward their cabin. She had never seen him look so tired or hurting so much. He was broken, like a horse, drained of resistance and unable to fight any more.

He only saw her when he stepped onto the porch and looked at the door.

"Mildred?"

She looked into his eyes. They were red and filled with tears. He stood in front of her, tears running down his cheeks. His handkerchief was in his hand.

"Mildred? They died. Them babies died. Effie cried and pushed all night but both of them babies was dead when they came out. You had to seem em. They was perfect. A little girl and a little boy. The prettiest little things you ever saw." He blew his nose. "A man shouldn't have to see that. And I think it is a sign from God. He killed them perfect babies because they came from sin, from the devil. I broke my vow to you and God was punishing me for doing it. I know that's what the preacher would say."

He lifted his arms and Mildred knew what he wanted. She stood and let him fall into her. It felt to Mildred like he was bent double over her, his chest on her shoulder and his face dripping tears down her back. If she had been stronger she could have lifted him up and carried him in the door. He sobbed so hard she thought he would lose his breath.

He had just come from seeing his own babies die. His own babies coming out from inside another woman. Not his wife. Not her. She wanted to hurt him but knew she couldn't hurt him more than he was already feeling. He needed her now.

She had to love him more, not less. Take care of him better than his mother could have, if she had been around. She needed to show him that no matter what he did or what he needed she would forgive it and be there for him. That was all she could do. That was all she knew how to do. Have faith that he would see it and that it would change him. Stick with him and love him right through it. The preacher called this *grace*.

1936

Mildred felt the first pang when she bent to add wood to the cook stove. It was too early in the day to build up the fire for cooking supper but she added small pine logs to try to keep the house warm. She had agreed with Carlos earlier that morning, when he came in from milking the cows, the steam still rising from the milk pail, that this might be the coldest day either of them had ever known.

The women she knew told her that she wouldn't make it her full nine months. They said it looked like she was having twins and that she was just too little. Mildred didn't know what to expect. It was her first baby.

She thought at first it was just another twinge of pain in her back, like the ones she had been having the last month or so. But as she straightened herself on one of their ladderback chairs, and placed the balls of her hands on her hips, she knew that this pain was different and that it wasn't going to get any better. She pulled tight the quilt around her shoulders and took tentative steps to the front door. She opened it just a crack and pushed her face into the knife of icy wind that came through the opening. She looked up the hill toward the Langstons' house. Thick smoke poured from the broad stone chimneys at the ends of the house. She saw no one outside. Her eyes followed the ridge at the top of the hill to the large barn. She wondered if Carlos might be inside or if he had gone into town with Mister Langston.

"Missus Langston?"

Mildred called out, the steam of her breath blowing back onto her face.

"Missus Langston?"

The sounds of her shouts seemed to die in the cold air before they even left the porch. She closed the door, walked back to the wood stove, and sat in the hard seat of the rocking chair at its side. The pain began to fade and Mildred closed her eyes.

Another searing pain just beneath her ribs woke Mildred with a start. She tried to take a deep breath, but the pain cut it short. She held the arms of the chair and slowly rocked with a slight movement of her ankles and feet. The pain ebbed as she held her breath.

She looked at the door when she heard the sound of heavy treads on the steps and porch. Carlos rushed in and closed the door quickly behind him.

"Goddamn it's cold out there. That ice has done covered everything a half-inch thick. Them little pine trees down by the creek are bent over and the tops are done froze to the ground. After we chopped holes in all the troughs so the stock could get some water, Mister Langston told us all to go home, said it was no use trying to work when it was this cold. Said he didn't want us all laid up in the bed next week sick from it either." Carlos unbuttoned his coat as he made his way to the wood stove. He looked at Mildred for the first time. "Sugar, what's wrong?"

"Carlos, I think it's time for the baby."

"You sure?"

"I think so."

"Well, what can I do for you?"

"Go get Missus Langston to stay with me while you go get Aunt Neva. She said she'd help me when the time come."

Carlos rushed around the room, as if he were looking for something without remembering exactly what. "Can I get anything for you before I go? You wanna sit there or go to the bed? You want me to build up the fire?"

Mildred looked toward him and began to cry.

"No, just go get Missus Langston and bring her down here for me, then go to Appleby. Please hurry."

"Okay, Sugar."

Carlos patted Mildred on the top of her head, walked to the front door, buttoned his coat and went out.

When Missus Langston got to the cabin, Mildred had made it across the room and was leaning with her bottom against the edge of the bed, doubled over in pain, her face bright red with beads of sweat on her brow. Her chin rested on her chest and her fingers were locked beneath the bulge of the child.

She looked up at Missus Langston, who closed the door behind her and shed layers of clothing as she crossed the room. "Missus Langston, I think I'm bleeding down there. It feels real wet."

Missus Langston held Mildred's wrists and pulled her hands away. "You are just fine, Honey. You're not bleeding. That's just the water the baby was swimming in that's coming out. It's supposed to happen that way. That just means that your baby is ready. Let's just get you up here on this bed."

The older woman helped Mildred lift herself onto the bed. Mildred lay back against the thin pillows Missus Langston gathered behind her shoulders and head.

Missus Langston took off Mildred's shoes and socks, pulled her dress up over her head and off, and covered her with the sheet, two quilts, and a blanket, all the bedclothes the couple owned.

"You just sit tight, Mildred. Mister Langston took Carlos in the truck to get your aunt in Appleby. Them roads is all iced up, but in the truck they'll be back shortly. It ain't that far. And I'll be with you until then."

Carlos heard the screams as he stepped out of the truck in front of the Langstons' house. At first, he thought that Missus Langston had moved Mildred up the hill to her own house, but as he turned the corner of the big house he could tell the sounds were coming from the cabin down the hill.

Mildred's Aunt Neva rushed past Carlos. "Oh, Lord. That child must be dying, crying like that."

Carlos watched as the old woman ran down the hill, jumped onto the porch and slammed the door behind her. He rushed after her. As he walked up the steps, Missus Langston came out of the front door.

"Carlos, your wife's aunt says for you to come on up to the house with me and wait. She wants me to send for Doctor Snyder in town. There is something wrong. The baby ain't coming right."

Carlos shook his head and followed Missus Langton back up the hill to her house. Later, he sat in front of the fireplace in the parlor of the Langston home, thinking. Although he had known the Langston family his entire life, he felt uncomfortable there and sat on the edge of the seat, not letting his back touch the fine fabric of the chair. Carlos was warmer here than he had been in weeks. Mister Langston turned on the radio to cover the sounds from down the hill. A small calf, born to one of Mister Langston's prized Brahman cows, slept in a child's playpen in the corner. Mister Langston sat in the chair opposite Carlos.

"My wife almost kicked me out of the house this morning when I brought that thing in. Said a parlor wasn't no place for a calf. But she gave in when I told her it would die for certain if we left it without its momma in the cold. She's not making enough milk. And what is she doing having a calf this early in the year? She must have been bred the first thing last spring."

Both men stood as they heard the approach of cars. They walked to the window to see Mister Langston's son turn off the main road and into the lane that led to the house. He was followed by the doctor in a new Ford coupe.

Although Carlos knew of Doctor Snyder and had surely seen him from a distance in town, he had never called on him for his services. And he had no idea how he would pay him for his help. Carlos walked outside and approached the tall thin man, as the doctor removed a large leather satchel from the rumble seat of his car.

Mister Langston nodded toward Carlos. "This is Carlos Dews, my new hand. It's his wife who is having trouble with her first baby."

The two men shook hands and Carlos pointed down the hill. "She's down there in the cabin where we live, down the hill behind the house."

Carlos led the way as all three men walked down to the cabin. The screaming had stopped. Carlos mounted the steps and knocked lightly on the door.

They heard quick treads inside, then the door opened just a crack. "Neva, I've got the doctor here to see her. How is she doing?"

Neva widened the crack in the door and looked at the three men. "Carlos, you and the doctor come on in quick, I don't want any of this heat I've built up in here to get out. The poor thing was just a-shiverin, I guess from all the sweatin she's been doing. But she is resting easy now between the pains. At least for a minute, anyway." Neva turned to the doctor. "I sure hope you can do something for her, Doctor Snyder. I've been praying for you to get here safe through all that ice and for you to be able to do something to help her when you got here. I've never seen a girl hurt so much in having a little one. I've done about all I can do. This one seems determined to come out ass backwards. I've got a pot of hot water on the stove and a bunch of rags all torn up and soaking, if you need em to sop up any blood."

"I'll sure do what I can for her, Missus Scogin."

Doctor Snyder walked to the side of the bed where Mildred lay on her back, covered to her chin, a valley of fabric sagged between her raised knees. The doctor touched her shoulder as he leaned over her. "Missus Dews, I'm Doctor Snyder. I'm gonna try and help you with the baby. Do you mind if I take a look?"

Mildred rolled her head from side to side on the sweat-soaked pillow. The doctor lifted the cover at the foot of the bed, gathering it on the top of her knees.

He knew immediately that the girl's aunt was correct and that the baby was breech. But he had never seen a baby so large wedged within the birth canal of a woman so small. Only one side of the baby's bottom was projecting through the vulva and it alone filled the space normally dilated for a baby's head. Pushed out alongside the buttock was the baby's swollen purple scrotum. He pushed on her stomach then attempted to insert his fingers beside the baby. He couldn't. There was no space left.

Carlos and Neva watched as the doctor completed the examination, then covered Mildred's legs and feet. He removed a syringe and vial from his bag and gave Mildred an injection in her arm. He turned back toward Carlos and Neva.

"Missus Scogin, could you come over here and make sure that she doesn't need anything while Mister Dews and I talk for just a minute?"

Doctor Snyder put his arm around Carlos's shoulder and walked him to the front door. They stood facing it, their faces only inches from each other.

"Mister Dews, I'm sorry, but I have some bad news," Doctor Snyder whispered. "Your wife is mighty small and that baby she is trying to have is awfully big. That wouldn't necessarily be a problem, but this baby is coming out breech. That means instead of coming out head first, it's doubled up and coming with its little rear end first."

Carlos winced. "But Doctor Snyder, there must be something you can do to help it along, ain't there? I know when a cow is having trouble with a calf that you can tie a rope to the calf's leg and pull it out. Can't you do something like that?"

"Well, Mister Dews, it's not that easy. This baby is much too big and your wife is just too small. If we tried something like that then your wife could hemorrhage, bleed to death, and the baby would more than likely die in the process too. You could lose them both."

Doctor Snyder looked over his shoulder to where Mildred's Aunt Neva sat on the edge of the bed, patting Mildred's forehead and holding her hand.

"Mister Dews, there is really only two options we have at this point, and neither one of them is good. Given where things are now, this baby is not gonna be born regular. We're either gonna have to make more room for the baby to come out, and I'm not sure your wife would survive this, or we can use a tool I have, a string saw, and cut the baby up so we can get it out of her. Now, this option would almost certainly save your wife's life, but there could be damage and she might not be able to have any other children. I know you are a farming man and have been around animals giving birth all your life, so you can understand how these choices have to be made sometimes."

Carlos looked into Doctor Snyder's eyes. "Doctor, this is our first youngin, we been married for almost six years now and this is the first time she's made it this far with one. You sure there ain't nothing else you could do that would save em both? And it's a boy, ain't it? I could see its balls."

"Yes, Mister Dews. But we don't have much time. The sooner we decide and do something, the better."

Carlos leaned closer to the doctor and spoke into his ear. The doctor nodded then walked to the side of the bed and rested his hand on Neva's shoulder. She stood and joined Carlos at the door. As the doctor leaned over and spoke to Mildred, Carlos talked with Neva.

"No, Carlos, I can't let you do that and I know Mildred won't either. You can't kill that baby. If it's the Lord's will for this to happen then that's the way it's gotta be. You can't just cut up that baby like that. We just gotta pray for something to be done."

"Neva, the doctor says that's all there is to do."

Neva sank to her knees on the floor in front of Carlos, her hands clasped together and her eyes toward the ceiling. Her lips moved in silent prayer as she began to crawl on her knees across the floor toward the bed.

Carlos walked to the side of the bed and stood behind the doctor.

"Mister Dews, I don't think you want to be here for this, but I will need some help. Missus Scogin, can you stay here to assist me?"

Neva interrupted her prayers and stared up at the doctor. "There ain't no way I'm helping you to do nothing if it's gonna hurt that baby. I won't be a part of it. It's the Lord's will and that's the way it is."

The doctor turned away from her. "Mister Dews, do you think Missus Langston would come down and help? And could you send her back with the black case in the floor board of the rumble seat in my car?"

"I can sure ask her. And if she won't, I'll bring the bag back down and help you myself."

As Carlos turned to go, Neva lunged toward him, throwing her arms around his legs.

"Carlos, you can't do this. You've gotta trust in the Lord. Let me have a chance. Just give me a few minutes. God will help us if we just ask Him. Get down here with me. Get down on your knees and ask the Lord God for His help in saving both of em."

Carlos looked toward the doctor, who was placing instruments from his case on the small table at the side of the bed. He looked down at the woman then up to Carlos. He shook his head.

"Aunt Neva, the doctor says there is no other way," Carlos said, lifting Neva to her feet. "And if we wait any more, they both could die. Do you want that to happen?"

"Give me just five minutes, please. She's been paining for hours and she is still trying her best. Five more minutes, that's all I ask. Let me talk with the Lord."

"Doc, let's let her do her praying, at least a few minutes."

The doctor threw the instrument in his hand back into his bag. "Mister Dews, now I'm a religious man myself, so I understand the strength of Missus Scogin's faith, but sometimes we have to make hard decisions that might not seem right, but that we have to trust are the right thing to do. We both know there is only one thing to be done. I'm going up to the car for my other bag myself, and when I come back we have to do something. We just can't wait."

The doctor walked out the front door.

Neva walked to the end of the bed and dropped to her knees. She slipped her hands under the ends of the covers and took hold of

Mildred's feet. She closed her eyes and began to pray. Carlos stood by the bed and held his wife's hand. Mildred looked up at him. He sat next to her and put his hand behind her head.

"Oh, Carlos, I think I'm about to die. I can't take this for much more."

Carlos looked down the length of the bed to Aunt Neva. She lifted the quilts and blankets and climbed beneath them, her shoulders between Mildred's ankles and her head a bulge between Mildred's thighs. She began to moan and wail, speaking in the tongues and chatter Carlos heard when he went to church with his wife's family. The old woman's voice sounded like the auctioneer at the sale barn but with words Carlos couldn't understand.

Carlos later said that, from beneath the weight of the bedclothes, he saw the baby turn, point, and move and shift as he watched. Mildred would say she felt the baby turn over and around inside her, just like it was hit with a bolt of lightning.

Aunt Neva emerged from under the covers, her eyes wide, adjusting to the new light. "Carlos, go fetch the doctor, that baby is a-comin now and Mildred's bleedin some."

By the time Carlos and the doctor returned, the baby had been born. When they walked in the door, Mildred was holding it in her arms and Aunt Neva was down between her knees with a dish pan and rags.

Neva turned to the doctor. "The bleeding was just about done when she passed the afterbirth. It came out real fast. She seems to be doing fine now, but I'd feel better if you took a look. Since you are here, anyway."

Carlos turned and walked back out the front door and into the cold. He came back with a large icicle in his hand. He walked to the side of the bed and broke it into two pieces. Mildred took one piece and began to suck on it, savoring the pure water, soothing her parched lips and throat. Carlos held the other piece of ice against the palm of his newborn son, the tiny hand contracting with the cold.

Mildred looked into Carlos's eyes. She was certain that the baby
and the miracle of his birth would change Carlos forever.

May 1946

Beamon, wearing his Army uniform, rested on a cot on the front porch. "Mildred, Mister Foshay is here."

Mildred came to the screen door drying her hands on a dish towel. Mister Foshay stood in front of his car at the bottom of the porch steps. "Why, Mister Foshay, Carlos and the boy are down in the back field if you are looking for him. You know my brother Beamon, don't you?" Mildred pointed down the porch toward her brother. "He's staying here with us while he gets over the mumps. You had the mumps, Mister Foshay? I sure hope so. You don't want to catch em. They let him come here to get better so he wouldn't pass it on to any other of the boys on the base. Plus, he's about to get his discharge anyway."

Mildred wanted to keep Mister Foshay out on the porch if she could, just in case Carlos came in early from the field. "My daddy wouldn't let him come home to get better," she continued. "Said he didn't want him spreading it to him and his new wife Lucille, since neither of them ever had the mumps. You know how my daddy is."

Mister Foshay took off his hat and stepped up onto the front porch. "Yes, Mam, I do, and I do know Beamon. Howdy, son. Mildred, I can't believe that your littlest brother is big enough to have served in the Army."

"Well, he is." Mildred remained behind the screen door. "You want me to tell Carlos something for you? Something about what you want him to do next or something?"

Mildred remembered what Carlos said the last time he came home from the fields and found Mister Foshay sitting with her in the kitchen drinking coffee: "if I ever come home again and find you in the house alone with my wife I'll kill you."

The words sounded funny. She knew Carlos used the word house instead of my house or our house because Carlos knew who actually owned the house. They lived on Mister Foshay's land in Mister Foshay's house, and Carlos drove Mister Foshay's pickup truck. By saying something like that to Mister Foshay, Carlos risked them having to move again. Carlos's temper, what people in the county called that damned Dews meanness, had already caused them to have to leave the Langston place a few months before.

"No, I don't have anything to talk to Carlos about. I just thought I would stop by and check on things. See how yawl were getting along. See if you needed anything for the house."

"No, I think everything is just fine. Thank you for asking, though." Mildred rested her right hand on the thin spring that held the screen door closed.

"Well, I sure would like some of that sweet, strong coffee you make, even if it's left from breakfast. I just can't get those girls of mine to make coffee like Missus Foshay used to make, God rest her soul."

Mildred looked back down the hall toward the kitchen. "I might have a little I could heat up for us all. You wanna have a seat out here with Beamon and I'll bring it out here to you?"

"If it's all the same to you, Miss Mildred, I'd rather sit in the kitchen and talk and drink the coffee with you."

Mildred exchanged a glance with Beamon. "Mister Foshay, you remember last time we had coffee?"

"What do you mean? How old Carlos got so mad when I was over here? He didn't mean nothing. Was just tired after a long day behind that mule. I think he was maybe even just joking about that."

Mister Foshay stepped to the door, opened the screen, and pushed by Mildred. His large belly, covered by the plaid vest he always wore, pushed against Mildred's side.

Mildred followed as he walked down the center hallway toward the kitchen at the back of the house. He pulled out one of the chairs from under the table, sat down, spreading his legs wide, his round stomach resting between his thighs. Mildred turned to the stove and began to heat the coffee.

"I've been wanting to talk to you about something for a while. I want you to know that some of us know how Carlos treats you and your boy, how he works you so hard, and how he goes with other women. My sister wanted me to tell you that we could help you out, if you need it or if you ever need to leave. I would even hire you to work for me in my house."

"Mister Foshay—"

"Now Mildred, don't get me wrong. We just want you to know that people would take care of you and your boy, if you need us to."

"Mildred?" Beamon called from the front porch. Mildred looked past Mister Foshay, down the hall and out the front door. "Mister Foshay, Carlos is here."

Carlos drove the pickup to the front of the house, their son on the seat next to him. He jumped from the cab of the pickup truck. "Boy, you stay right there in that truck." He threw open the screen door and came into the hallway.

Mildred expected Carlos to rush down the hall toward the kitchen but instead he turned into their bedroom at the front of the house. "Mister Foshay, you better run out the back here. I think Carlos is gone after his gun."

"Mildred, we can be reasonable here. Carlos won't do nothing to me."

Carlos came down the hallway toward the kitchen, his double-barreled shotgun in his hands. "You sorry son of a bitch. I warned you the last time. You better get out of this house."

Mildred backed against the wall beside the stove, her palms flat against the clapboard wall.

Mister Foshay put both his palms on the table and stood. He turned to face Carlos. "Now, Carlos, be reasonable. Miss Mildred and I were just going to sit and visit and drink some of her good coffee. Do you think we'd be up to anything with her brother sitting up there on the front porch?"

"You better get out of this fucking house. Now." Carlos pointed the barrels of the gun toward the back door. "Out that way. You ain't gonna walk back through this house."

Mister Foshay walked out the door and down the back steps. Carlos followed him and stood on the top step. Mildred stood behind the screen door. When he reached the smooth dirt yard, Mildred saw Mister Foshay stop, push his shoulders back and turn back to face Carlos.

"Carlos Dews, just wait a goddamned minute. I think you have forgotten who owns this house and who it is that you work for. You can't talk to me that way on my own place."

"I ain't forgot a damn thing. You may own this house and the whole goddamn place, but as long as I live in this house I can say who can visit with my wife when I'm not at home." Carlos lifted the butt of the gun to his shoulder and pointed the barrels at Mister Foshay's face.

"Carlos, listen to me." Mister Foshay stepped to the side and lifted his right hand to push the gun away.

As Mister Foshay's hand passed in front of the gun, Carlos pulled the double trigger, firing both barrels.

Mister Foshay's hand disappeared in a cloud of pink and white mist. Only the ragged edges of his wrist and thumb remained.

After the recoil from the shot Carlos didn't move. He turned his head back toward Mildred. "I told the son of a bitch to leave."

Mildred ran out the door and down the steps. Mister Foshay sat on the hard soil at the bottom of the steps, the stump of his hand held to his chest, blood oozing down the front of his vest.

Mildred knew what this meant. They would have to move again, at least. Carlos might go to jail. And if Mister Foshay died then Carlos would go to Huntsville and hang or die in the chair. And she knew what she would have to do now. She would get this man to a doctor, or a doctor to him. She would pack up the house and find them a new place to live. She would promise that Carlos would change, that he wouldn't do it again or any more. She would find a lawyer and beg him to keep Carlos out of jail or out of the chair, and to do it not knowing if he would ever get paid for his work. She would have to take care of their boy and take care of Beamon with the mumps and do all the little things and the big things. And she would make sure that her boy didn't turn out like his daddy. But she was afraid he was already lost. Just like his daddy and his daddy's daddy.

Late that night, when she was trying to go to sleep, she thought, deep down, that perhaps she deserved what she got with Carlos. Maybe God was giving her all this trouble, this burden to love this impossible man, for what she had done to that baby when her mother died.

May 1950

Mildred convinced Carlos to let her and their son break off from working in the field and go to the house an hour early. But that didn't mean that they had less work to do. As she and the boy followed their teams of mules from the field back to the barn, the handles of their tin lunch pails lining Mildred's arm, she made a list in her mind. She didn't want to forget anything. If she did anything wrong, Carlos might change his mind and not let them go. She had to anticipate anything he might need from her while she was gone.

After unhitching the mules and turning them into the lot, she had to feed and pen the chickens, milk the cow and feed the calf, cook Carlos something to eat and leave it on the table covered with a dish towel, clean up the house, heat and draw her own bath, bathe, heat and draw the boy a bath, then make sure that there was plenty of hot water so Carlos could have a bath when he came in from working. Finally she had to turn down the bed and tune the radio to Carlos's favorite station. She knew she had two hours to do it all before he came in from the field.

"I see your daddy coming, go meet him at the barn and tell him we're leaving. If he needs anything he better ask for it now. But don't tell him I said that."

Mildred gathered her things, stepped off the porch, and began walking down the long lane to the main road. She wanted to be out of the house before he came in. She wondered exactly why he was allowing them to go. Maybe he had plans to meet up with one of his women, to sneak back over to the Williams place, just to check on things, as he always said. Tonight, she wouldn't care if he did see another woman.

Carlos had allowed them to go but wouldn't let them take the pickup truck, or even a team of mules and the rubber-tired wagon. Mildred was prepared to walk the five miles to town, but was certain one of their neighbors would come along and offer them a ride, since almost everyone from the surrounding farms would be going into town for the singing.

Before she and Carlos had walked a quarter mile, they heard the rumble of an approaching truck and turned to see the red cloud of dust thrown up behind the pickup of the Stanaland family. Mister and Missus Stanaland rode in the cab of the truck, their three children in the back. Mildred and Carlos moved to the side of the road as the truck stopped beside them, the cloud of dusk enveloping them all. Missus Stanaland leaned out the open passenger window.

"Mildred, you and the boy walking to Garrison for the singing?"

"Yes, Mam, we are. You know how much I love Hank Williams."

"Well, get on up in here with us."

Missus Stanaland slid across the seat toward her husband and Mildred climbed into the truck. Carlos jumped over the tailgate into the back with the other children.

Mildred took a deep breath and began to relax as the gate to their place disappeared behind them. She was afraid that Carlos might run down the lane and say that he had changed his mind, that she and Carlos couldn't go to town after all, or that he had forgotten something that she must do before nightfall. He always called Hank Williams "that damned brokeback hillbilly boy," and he hated when she listened to his show on the radio.

Mister Stanaland turned to Mildred. "Mildred, what field are yawl working now?"

"We're over in that patch behind the ridge, down toward the creek. Even though Mister Hart didn't tell him to, Carlos wants to break it up one more time this fall. Says it will keep the weeds down and make the plowing easier in the spring."

Mister Stanaland sucked on his teeth. "Sometimes I think that man is gonna work you and your boy to death."

"I know it. He just made our boy stop going to school. He was headed into the seventh grade this year, too. And he had passed all his grades so far. Superintendent Francis even came out to the field and tried to talk Carlos into letting him go back to school, said the boy was already big enough in the sixth grade, that he was sure he would make a mighty good football player. Said he was smart, too. But Carlos just sent Mister Francis on his way. Threatened to get his gun. Said Carlos was his son and that he would decide how to raise him."

The town square in Garrison had been transformed for the show. It was free of cars, lights had been strung between buildings on either side of the square, and hay bales had been placed in rows as seats. A long trailer from the Bartons' saw mill was parked across one end of the square as a stage. A banner hung across it: *KRRE Radio presents Hank Williams and The Cowboys.*

Mildred insisted that they sit near the front, Carlos at her side. She knew the words to every song Williams sang, and during the concert she couldn't take her eyes off him.

Mildred could tell the singer was in pain. She saw how he stood with his right hip pushed to the side and how his right shoulder turned inward toward his heart. She imagined resting her hands on his body where it hurt, helping to relieve his pain. And she knew his heart suffered too. The songs he sang were filled with pain and suffering. This man's heart had been broken too many times. And for as many reasons as she could imagine. But Mildred knew she could heal it. Given the chance.

After the concert the singer and his band walked down the steps at the end of the stage and stood to meet the people who waited in a line that stretched around the town square. Mildred didn't join until there were only a few people left in the line. She wanted to be the last in line to talk to him.

As she strained to hear what the singer said to those in line in front of them, Mildred grew nervous. She didn't know what she would say. She wanted him to understand that they were two of a kind. That she knew exactly what he felt.

The family in front of them finished talking to the singer and turned to walk away. He spoke first. "Howdy, little lady. Who is this fine boy with you tonight?"

"This is my boy. Carlos."

"He may be your boy, Mam, but he looks as big as any man here. And I'm sure, Mam, that you aren't old enough to have a boy this big." The singer extended his hand to Carlos. "How you doing, son?"

"Just fine, sir. Thank you."

"And what is your name, Mam?"

"I'm Mildred. Mildred Dews. I sure did enjoy your singing tonight, Mister Williams. And I wanna tell you that."

Jaynelle Phillips, one of the daughters of a sharecropper on the Ramsey place, ran to Mildred's side. "Mildred, Daddy just come from over at the Lunsford place. He said Mary Alice is having her baby and she is crying for you. She said you done helped her with her other seven babies and she said she ain't having this one without you. I promised Daddy I'd let you know. You better get out there to her."

"But Jaynelle, I'm here afoot. Me and Carlos rode into town with the Stanalands. We was going to ride back with them, or walk back home or catch a ride with somebody else if we could."

The singer stepped between the two women. "Mam, what direction is this place you need to get to to help with this baby?"

"It's about ten miles south, about halfway between here and Nacogdoches. It's just off the highway at the Holly Springs junction."

"Well, me and the boys are headed to Nacogdoches now. I could give you a ride down there, if you can wait a few minutes while we finish packing up."

"No, Mister Williams, I couldn't ask you to do that."

"It wouldn't be a problem at all. We're going that way anyway."

Missus Stanaland stepped forward and squeezed Mildred's arm. "Mildred, you go on with Mister Williams, we'll take the boy home and tell Carlos where you are."

"Carlos, you tell your daddy that I'll be with Mary Alice until that baby comes. Tell him I'll get a ride home from somebody as soon as it's born. Or I'll get Lee to bring me home, if he can leave Mary Alice. But it might be sometime tomorrow."

The singer led Mildred to a car parked at the end of the stage.

"This sure is a fine car."

"Yes, Mam, it is. It's almost brand new. A 1949 Cadillac. And the top comes down, a convertible."

The members of the singer's band stood smoking between the Cadillac and a Buick with a trailer attached parked next to it. "Mildred, this here is Bob, Hilly, Jerry, and Don. Boys, this is Miss Mildred Dews."

The men nodded in unison.

"I'm gonna drive this little lady out to this other lady's house who's having a baby. I'll meet up with you fellas down at the Y, you know where this here highway hits up with the Henderson highway just north of Nacogdoches. Yawl wait on me at the café at that little motel that sits right there. I'll be on down as quick as I can."

The band members exchanged grins, tossed away their cigarettes, and piled into the Buick.

Mildred looked back at the crowd still standing in the town square as the singer turned onto the highway and drove south out of town.

"Mister Williams, I sure do appreciate this. And Mary Alice just won't believe that you brought me out to her. We've listened to you on the radio so many times together."

"It's no problem, Mam. I know what hard times is like and I welcome the chance to help somebody in need."

"I sure do appreciate it."

Mildred looked across the seat at the singer.

"Mister Williams, you know, I feel like I already know you. I've known of you since Mister Roy Acuff used to call you the Singing Kid. That was back during the war. Three of my brothers was overseas fightin and one of them is still overseas, in Japan. He stayed on in the Army after the war. 'You're Gonna Change or I'm Gonna Leave' is my favorite of your songs. But just when I decide which is my favorite I hear your next one and like it the best."

"Well, Mam, I might just need you to run my fan club for me, or at least keep me straight about when I done things. I think you might know more about me than I do about myself."

"Do you know that old song by Jimmie Rogers, 'My Mother Was a Lady'?"

"Yes, Mam, I do."

"I sure wish you would sing that one sometime. And do you know that song about the Titanic sinking?" The singer nodded. "My momma used to sing that one to us all the time before she died. She would sing it to us when she was rocking us to sleep as babies. But don't get me wrong, I like when you sing your own songs best."

"That's mighty nice of you."

"And when you sing by yourself."

"Do you mean you don't like when I sing with my Miss Audrey?

"Yes, sir. Mister Williams. How did you get down here from up in Nashville so fast? I just heard your show from Nashville last night on the radio."

"Well, Mam, we make a record of the show when we are in Nashville and they play it on the radio like we was doing it live. We was just over in Shreveport last night."

"Well, your Health and Happiness Show is already just about my favorite thing on the radio. That and the Opry and the Louisiana Hay Ride. I try not to miss em every week. And I remember the first time I heard you on the Opry. That show went on and on. Them folks made you sing the whole show almost over again."

"Yes, Mam, they made me sing six other songs. They call em encores. That's the most anybody's had to do at the Opry before. And we had to drive to Memphis that night after that show too. I was near hoarse the next day from all that singing." The singer reached under his seat and pulled out a whiskey bottle. "You mind if I have a drink?"

"No, not a bit."

"This old back of mine hurts me so much I just got to have something to cut through the pain a little. And sometimes I miss Audrey and our baby so much I can't stand it. This helps me with that too. I get awfully tired of all this traveling around. But I got to do it. That's the way they tell me you sell them records. Our baby just turned one a few days ago. Little Hank. Randall Hank. Just like me. He's a junior."

"Me and my husband named our boy after his daddy too. But my husband don't like using juniors, so we gave him the second name of Weldon, after my oldest brother, the one over in Japan."

The singer passed the bottle to Mildred. She took a long drink and passed it back to him. "And I sure do like your new radio show. All them songs about heartache and pain. But my husband sure don't like it. He won't even stay in the house when I'm listening to it. Can you imagine such a thing? A man jealous of a radio show."

"Well, he wouldn't be the first husband to not like me."

The singer downshifted the Cadillac as they began to coast down a pine covered hill.

Mildred pointed into the distance. "See that clearing on the top of that little rise over there? Where that big oak tree is? The big one you can see against the sky?"

"Yes, Mam."

"Looks like a pretty place for a house up there, don't it?"

"Yeah, it sure does."

"Well, that's because there used to be a big house up there. Now it's the saddest place I know of. There was two little old ladies, sisters, that lived up on that hill in a big house their daddy built for them when he figured out they weren't ever gonna get married. They were the Langston sisters. Everybody called them the Langston girls, even when they got to be old women. One fall, they raked the leaves of that big oak tree in front into a big pile and set out to burn them. But the long dress tail of one of them ladies caught afire, and when the other one ran up to help her put it out, her dress caught too. Then one of em must have run up on the porch with her dress afire, cause the fire spread to the porch and burned the whole house down. Both of em died right there, too. My daddy was passing by when it happened, he was taking a load of sweet potatoes into town to sell, and he was the first to get there. Said he couldn't do a thing. Just pulled em out of it the best he could then just had to watch and wait until their brother and a doctor got there later. I've always thought that story might make a good, sad song."

"Yes, Mam, it might."

"Now see this road coming up here to the right? Just as you start up the hill. You need to turn right there. The Lunsford place is just up that road a little ways. I sure hope Mary Alice ain't having no trouble with this baby. I sure had trouble when Carlos was born. Liked to died. Made it so I couldn't have no more babies."

They turned onto the narrow country road and crossed a plank bridge over a creek, climbed a short hill, and stopped in front of the Lunsford house. Three hounds came from under the front porch to sniff the car's tires.

Mildred reached across the singer's legs and turned off the car's headlights. She rested her hand on the steering wheel then let her hand drop to his thigh. He turned to look at her. She looked into his eyes.

"Mister Williams, I want you to take me with you. I could take care of you better than anybody ever has. I could travel around with you. Take me with you. Just back out real quick and let's go. Take me with you. I can do anything. I could cook for you. I could take care of your suits. And I don't mean no disrespect for Miss Audrey. I could take care of you better than any woman ever has. I could even drive for you. I could rub liniment on that bad back of yours whenever it got to hurting you. And I don't mean sleeping with you or nothing. You know what it's like. I know where you come from. We are the same."

"Now, Miss Mildred—"

"This man I'm married to is gonna work us to death. We only have the one boy and my old man drives us harder than he does the mules in the field, always on me and Carlos about something. It's like he expects the same work out of us as a big family. He won't let us rest, says we're lazy if we're not doing something all the time. Keeps us running all the time, wanting to plant more and more acres every year. Tells Mister Hart he don't need to hire nobody else on the place, that we can do it all. And there are just the three of us to do it. And he runs around on me. I've caught him so many times with other women. I'm at the end of my rope. When we first married I thought he was just right for me, and that if there was ways he wasn't I could change him. I used to think I could change him, but I've just about decided I can't. I always thought that if I just kept on loving him, he would finally appreciate it and stop his running around and overworking us, but I'm beginning to think it ain't gonna happen."

The singer shifted on the seat to face her. "Now, Miss Mildred, you know I can't take you with me. You are mighty pretty, and I don't want you to take this wrong, but you need to take care of your boy, and I've got Miss Audrey and my new boy to worry about. What would Audrey say?"

Mildred tightened her grip on his leg, curling her fingers to clench the fabric of his pants above his knee. Tears ran down her cheeks.

"But Mister Williams, Hank, you don't understand. I sit and listen to your music on the radio all the time. I understand all the hurt and sorrow and meanness you sing about. I know it, and I know you. I know we can understand each other. If the songs you write are true then I know you better than anybody. I could prove it to you too, if you'd just give me a chance. I think it was a sign that I was there tonight at your show and you offered me this ride."

Mildred heard the squeal of the spring of the screen door and looked up to see Lee Lunsford walk out onto the porch holding a coal oil lamp, trying to see beyond it into the darkness.

"Mildred, is that you? Mary Alice needs you real bad!"

"I'll be right there, Lee. You go on back in to Mary Alice. I'll be right there."

The singer reached in front of Mildred and turned the chrome handle of her door and pushed it open.

"Now Mildred, you need to get in there and help your friend."

Mildred stepped out of the car into the dusty yard. She bent at the waist and buried her face in the fabric of her skirt, her head against her knees. She wiped the tears from her eyes with her skirt.

"Now, you listen to the Opry this Saturday, you hear? After we sing down in Huntsville tomorrow night and Houston on Thursday and Friday, we have to get back on up to Nashville for the Opry on Saturday. I promise I'll sing something just for you. You listen. You'll know which song it is. I won't need to say a thing about it."

The singer backed quickly into the road and drove away.

Mildred stood in the darkness and watched until the red taillights of the Cadillac disappeared into the night.

May 1950

Lois knew from the way Mister Hughes looked at her as she said her goodbyes to him and to her mother that he never wanted to see her again. Standing at the door to the bus, she had hugged her mother and saw him looking at her over her mother's shoulder.

She graduated from high school in Beaumont the year before, then moved with them to Houston and continued to live under his roof. Mister Hughes had developed a grudge against her. He followed her with his eyes whenever she entered a room and stared at her down the length of the dinner table each night. She was now the last of his wife's children still at home, Lois's two older brothers left home for the military as soon as they were old enough to enlist. Mister Hughes was her mother's fourth husband and was, as Lois heard him say, tired of raising other men's children.

Lois sat in the seat behind the bus driver, her purse on the seat next to her, her suitcase in the belly of the bus. She had made this trip many times before, but this one felt different.

As the sidewalks of downtown Houston gave way to highway 59 that took the bus due north into the piney woods of East Texas, and the gas station and furniture store signs gave way to tall pine trees lining the road, Lois couldn't help but think that things would be different the next time she saw Houston, if she ever saw Houston again.

She wondered if her trip to her grandparents' farm in Nacogdoches County was actually Mister Hughes's idea. Her mother said that her parents needed help on the farm, now that they were getting older, especially during the summer when so much canning and preserving was done. Since the war, the local people in the country who lived around them had turned cold and weren't as willing to help a family with a German name. But Lois thought her mother might see something else in the way Mister Hughes looked at her.

Lois never knew her own father. He died on a courtroom table from heart failure while serving jury duty when she was only two weeks old. Her mother and Mister Hughes didn't have any children and he wanted it that way.

Lois looked at herself in the mirror over the driver's head. Her hair bounced on her shoulders as the bus bumped between sections of the concrete highway.

Her mother couldn't understand why Lois hadn't been able to find a young man to propose to her, or at least date her seriously, since they moved to Houston. She was a smart girl. She graduated with a B average from high school, had worked at a five and dime store after school during her senior year, and had even thought about going to a business college and becoming a secretary. But her mother and Mister Hughes had refused to pay her tuition. They both wanted her to get married and get out of the house.

From the window of the bus Lois counted churches, the red brick Methodist and white clapboard Baptist. She looked ahead on the side of the highway for approaching steeples. The Freewill Baptist, the Primitive Baptist, the Church of Christ, the Church of God, the Missionary Baptist, the Assemblies of God, the Church of the Nazarene, the Jehovah's Witness, the Seventh Day Adventist, the Church of God in Christ, the Congregational Methodist, the United Methodist, the Lutheran, the Pentecostal, and the Presbyterian.

Lois's secret was that she knew she was filled with sin. She knew that there was evil in her heart. The preacher back in Beaumont had told her so on the day she was baptized. Every time a man or boy looked at her she knew the devil was inside her.

He stepped out of the room just long enough for Lois to change from her dress into the white robe. He had told her to take off all her clothes, including her bra and panties. You don't want your underthings to be wet after we're done, he had said.

The robe was wrinkled. She stood pulling down on it to remove the deep creases when he opened the door, without knocking, and walked back into the small room. She let go of the white cloth and crossed her arms beneath her breasts.

He was still wearing his white shirt and a tie but had put on rubber waders that came up to just beneath his underarms, held up by rubber suspenders that disappeared over his shoulders. His black hair was slicked back with oil. He walked over and stood in front of her.

"How old are you, Lois?"

She felt his stale breath on her face. "I turned sixteen at my last birthday."

"Good. Good. I was happy to see you come up the aisle during the invitation last Sunday. Your momma is a fine Christian woman and I welcome you and all her children into the fellowship of the Lord's church."

The choir in the church downstairs began to sing a hymn and they both turned their heads toward the small door on the other side of the room.

Just as I am, without one plea, but that thy blood was shed for me, and that thou bidd'st me come to thee, O Lamb of God, I come, I come.

"I asked Brother Bradford to have the choir sing all four verses of the hymn, to give us time to talk before we go down. We'll go on down when they finish. Will you join me in prayer? Kneel down."

Lois lifted the edge of the long robe and knelt on the pine wood floor in front of the preacher.

"I want to talk to you before we go down into the baptistery because I want you to know for sure that the Lord will wash you clean today. No matter how sinful you are, He will wash you clean of your sins and make you new. You will be reborn into the spirit of the Lord in just a few minutes."

Just as I am, and waiting not to rid my soul of one dark blot, to thee, whose blood can cleanse each spot, O Lamb of God, I come, I come.

He knelt in front of her and placed his hands on her shoulders. "I've been watching you for a while. I can feel the devil in you, girl. He has been speaking to me through you. I can hear his voice."

His right hand slid down her shoulder and his knuckles brushed across her left breast.

"See, he told me to do that just now. The devil spoke to me through you and told me to touch you that way. But don't worry. We're gonna take care of that in a few minutes downstairs."

Lois lowered her head and looked at the floor between his knees.

"Yes, the devil is telling me to do this. And this."

His right hand dropped to the edge of the white robe and disappeared under it.

"No. Please don't."

"You need to understand that this is what you and the devil do to men and boys. You can say no, but the devil in you tells us yes."

She gasped when his hand touched her knee under the robe. His hand followed her thigh.

Just as I am, though tossed about with many a conflict, many a doubt, fightings and fears within, without, O Lamb of God, I come, I come.

"The devil is in you. The evil down here draws us to you."

He patted the inside of her upper thigh with his right hand. His left hand rubbed the bulge at the crotch in the front of his waders.

"We men are weak. We are sinners too. It's your responsibility to keep the devil from speaking through you. The Lord and I can give you a new start today, but the devil will always be waiting for you. It is easy to let the sin back in. He will wait. The devil is patient. And this is your test."

He pushed his index fingers between her legs and inside her.

Lois gasped and closed her eyes.

"And if you ever tell anyone about what the devil made me do today, that will show that he has won, that your baptism didn't take and you have let the devil back in your life. When we wash you clean downstairs, if it works, then you won't even want to talk about this again."

Just as I am, thou wilt receive, wilt welcome, pardon, cleanse, relieve; because thy promise I believe, O Lamb of God, I come, I come.

The choir below fell silent.

He removed his hand from under the robe and passed his index finger slowly in front of his nose. He closed his eyes and shook his head. He opened the small door and flipped the light switch just inside. Yellow light filled the space beneath them and revealed the steep narrow staircase that disappeared into the water below. They walked down the stairs together and into the warm water.

"I baptize thee, in the name of the Father and of the Son and of the Holy Ghost."

When she joined him and the congregation in the church, her hair still wet, Brother Williams asked the congregation to come forward and lay their hands on her to confirm the spirit of the Lord in her.

She believed every word he had said.

Lois closed her eyes and rested her head on the bus window. She felt the vibration of the engine as she sped forward, away from the only home she had and toward her future. Or her end. Perhaps her mother was right. Lois didn't know what she wanted, didn't know where she wanted to be, didn't know who she was or why she was in the world. She knew only a few things for sure. She had worn out her welcome at home. Mister Hughes didn't want her under his roof any longer. Her mother thought she was trouble waiting to happen. Her grandparents needed her for her labor. And that she was only a thought or action away from letting the devil back inside her.

May 1950

Fusako wore the same suit she was wearing the day she and Weldon met, a tailored light wool jacket over a white shirt and a skirt of the same fabric. Her hair was down and it hung to her shoulders. Doctor Ito stood at her side and she held his arm with her left hand. In her right hand she held a small bouquet of flowers. Weldon and his friend Captain Harvey stood to her right, wearing their dress uniforms. They all faced the desk of the Army chaplain who stood behind it with an open book in his hands.

Fusako looked up at the red-haired chaplain and to the large clock on the wall behind him. She could hear the tick of the seconds as they passed. Whore. Whore. Whore. Whore. She knew the secretary outside the door to the office thought she was a whore. And she knew that all those they passed, from the time they entered the base and walked by all the buildings to the small metal one where the chaplain had his office, thought the same. They had all stared at her as she and Doctor Ito first wrote their names in a big book and waited for the guards to call Weldon, then the chaplain, to gain permission for them to walk through the gate onto the base.

And she knew that everyone in the town thought the same. Her own people thought the same. Whore. Whore. Whore. Whore.

She didn't understand all the words the chaplain used, although her English had improved in the five months since she and Weldon first met in the doctor's office. Doctor Ito hadn't questioned her sudden serious desire to speak English, thinking that her inability to speak with the soldiers in the office had finally driven her to take her studies seriously. Every night when she returned to his house and sat across the table from him for their dinner, Doctor Ito practiced conversation with her. He still had the books he'd used when he studied English before going to medical school in San Francisco. Doctor Ito would tell her stories in English about his time in the United States, about the Japanese family he lived with in the city, and how this family had given him a place to live, a new religion, and his wife. He told Fusako how difficult it had been to convince his new bride to return to the land her parents had left just twenty years before. He convinced her that their love and faith and work would hold them together and prevent her from missing her family an ocean away. And it had been so.

Weldon had practiced the vows with Fusako. She knew that all she had to do was repeat what the chaplain said, but she wanted to do it well. Weldon went first and she listened carefully as he repeated the vows after the chaplain. Then it was her turn. Weldon looked into her eyes as she repeated the words.

"I, Fusako Terao, take you, David Weldon Scogin, to be my lawfully wedded husband, to honor and obey, in sickness and in health, for richer or poorer, until death do us part."

As she repeated the words, she heard the beat of her heart in her ears. Whore, whore, whore, whore. She knew from the beginning that her own people, those who knew her story and how she had come to live with Doctor Ito, those who knew her best, would turn on her when they learned of her love for Weldon. They would think that she had betrayed her heritage, her family, her country, and her personal honor by loving the American soldier. They would be convinced that she had sold herself for the affection and food and supplies and escape the American had to offer. Although she knew this was not true, all her protestations and the acceptance by Doctor Ito would mean nothing to them. She would spend the rest of her life marked as a whore, one of those dishonored girls who had sacrificed all their value to the Americans.

After the ceremony on the base they would go to Doctor Ito's church where they would stand, dressed in borrowed ceremonial kimonos, to have photographs taken. They would stand on the steps as neighbors would walk by and stare.

She would walk through the streets of Kurume with the eyes of the townspeople on her, watching her every move as if to see if her shame made her walk differently or carry her bag in a different way. She knew they would point to her and say to their daughters, she is one of those. You don't want to be one of those. Shame. Shame. Shame. Shame.

She knew the only way to escape the shame of what she was doing was to leave her home, to transfer all her allegiances and hopes onto this man she had known now for only five months. To leave her country and Doctor Ito and trust that their new love for one another would be enough.

Fusako told Doctor Ito about Weldon a week after the couple first spoke. He was more concerned with how the people of the town would respond than about what it meant for Fusako to date an American soldier. Doctor Ito had lived in the United States, his wife was born there, so he had a realistic view of the Americans in their midst. Doctor Ito let them use the formal living room of his house for their dates. He didn't want them to have to meet at his office, and didn't want them to have to be seen together on the streets.

"You may now kiss the bride."

Fusako turned and looked up into Weldon's face. He bent over and kissed her. She broke away from the kiss and buried her face against the front of his jacket. Her face was red and hot. She felt the chill of one of the brass buttons of his jacket press into her cheek.

Fusako knew that with the words they had just spoken, a door had slammed behind her. A door she could not reopen herself and that would never be opened to her again. Her parents and brothers burned to ashes in an instant. Although she could not explain it to herself, she found a strange satisfaction in the comfort provided by a man from the country responsible for the death of her parents—and so many others, almost everyone she knew from her childhood. He was kind and he had a sad face, but that was not enough to explain her sacrifice.

When Fusako was a little girl, she had once looked through a crack in the garden fence at the side of their home. She heard cries from Mrs. Yamaguchi next door. When Fusako looked into their garden she saw Mrs. Yamaguchi on her knees in front of her husband. Mr. Yamaguchi slapped his wife. But instead of standing and running from him, Mrs. Yamaguchi leaned forward and pushed her face into her husband's stomach, between the open halves of the jacket of his business suit. With her face pressed against his stomach, Mr. Yamaguchi couldn't swing his arm and strike her face again. He put his hands on the back of her head and held her still. As Fusako watched through the crack in the fence, Mr. Yamaguchi lifted his wife to her feet and kissed her on the forehead.

She didn't run. Mrs. Yamaguchi pressed herself against the man who struck her. She pushed toward the source of her pain and it stopped. At least for a moment.

How could they be in love when they couldn't speak to each other if their dates, if the times they spent together could be called dates, were spent sitting across from one another on the tatami mats of the doctor's formal living room? They sat and had tea, exchanged glances and bows from the neck.

They began with few words. He called her pretty and she called him nice. They sat across the small low table and looked into each other's eyes. The room surrounding them disappeared. They stared until smiles erupted on their faces. Fusako marveled at the wrinkles that formed at the sides of Weldon's eyes when he smiled. And when he told her the name of where he was from she thought it sounded like Nagasaki.

He asked her to marry him after three months. He wanted to be sure they understood one another so he brought an interpreter with him, Captain Harvey, a Japanese-American soldier from the base. They sat on the floor across the table from one another, in Doctor Ito's front room. The interpreter sat at the end of the table.

Weldon spoke as if he had been saving all the stories of his life just for her. As if he had never had anyone to tell his stories to. He spoke quickly, as if their time was limited, and he looked at Captain Harvey to make sure he understood each word before waiting to hear his own words repeated into her language.

He told her about his family. He told her about all his brothers and sisters. He told her about his sister Mildred and how she was the best one of them all. He told her about his dead mother. He told her about his father, and how he seemed to hate his own children, how he and his brothers had welcomed the chance to fight in the war, to get away from him. And he told her that was why he decided to stay in the Army even after the war was over.

He told her about the place he grew up, about the rolling red clay hills—they called it Redland—covered by pine trees and the broad hot fields that had been cleared of pines to grow cotton.

And he told her of his love. How he didn't have the words to express it but that he felt it. How he knew the minute he first saw her that she was what he needed.

After a while Captain Harvey seemed to disappear and they sat looking at one another. As if the words that Captain Harvey spoke in Japanese were coming from deep within Weldon's body and were making their way to her ears without Weldon having to open his mouth.

When his stories were exhausted, he stopped and bowed his head. She did the same. They then both turned to Captain Harvey. Fusako poured them cups of cool water from a pitcher that sat between them. Then she began to talk.

Weldon marveled as she spoke. With the halting English they had used to speak with one another, he had never heard her speak with such fluency. He was amazed by the speed of the words that she spoke to Captain Harvey while looking directly at him.

She spoke of her family. She told about their ancient traditional wooden house with its garden in the center of the city. She told him about her parents, about her mother's walk and her father's cigarettes. She told of her older brothers, who pretended not to like her but would have died defending her. She told him of their lives before the war and their trips into the mountains and to see Doctor Ito and his wife. She told him about her time at school in the city. And she told him of the bomb. About school and hearing what had happened. About her walk to Doctor Ito's house.

She told him about the other soldiers and how she knew he was different. And she told him about what it was like to love him, to know that there was another person in the world that she would die for. And she told him of the sacrifice she had already made to be with him, about her own people and their special kind of hatred for women who loved the American soldiers.

Fusako pushed away from Weldon's chest and turned to Doctor Ito. She was embarrassed that the doctor had seen them kiss. Doctor Ito hugged her to him and whispered into her ear.

"You are free. You can fly away now. Your parents and brothers live in the wind and can follow you across the ocean. I know that place. Go there with Weldon and forget about this country and its people. You are good. We both know that. Go with my blessing and love."

June 1950

Lois was confused when the two Spivey girls stopped by her grand-parents' house on a Wednesday afternoon and asked her to go to the fire with them on Saturday night. They referred to the fire as if she would know what they were talking about. It was a fire for light, not heat. And it was at the church.

She knew the Spivey girls from previous visits to her grandpar-ents but didn't know them well. They were a few years younger, still in high school, but her grandfather wanted her to meet some of the young people nearby so she accepted the invitation. Since she'd arrived almost a month earlier, Lois hadn't left her grandparents' place. She was content to spend all her time cleaning the house and helping her grandmother can and preserve the summer fruit and vegetables.

When Saturday evening came, Lois took a hot bath in the galva-nized tub in the kitchen. She was dressed an hour before the Spivey girls arrived and waited for them on the front porch swing. Her dress was simple blue cotton with a wide belt of the same fabric. Loose pleats hung to just beneath her knees.

Lois felt self-conscious whenever she visited her grandparents. People stared at her. They could tell she was from the city by the way she dressed. They always said she wore the prettiest things even if what she wore was simple compared to the other girls back down in Houston. The girls in the country wore dresses made at home without slips and petticoats to lift their skirts and give their bodies shape. Their dresses made their shoulders and arms look thin and brittle and the skirts hung straight over their bodies and legs, giving them a pitiful look.

The fire took place beside the cemetery of the Arlam Baptist Church at an intersection of two country roads. Since the nearest picture show was forty miles away, the young people from the neighboring farms met at the church once a month. They would build a fire in the pit used for barbecuing during the annual cemetery and church reunion, stand around it and talk for hours. One of the boys would bring a washtub of ice or cold spring water filled with Nehi soda, Big Red, Nu Grape, and Coca-Cola. Someone would bring a watermelon when they were in season.

It was almost sunset when Lois and the Spiveys arrived at the church. The older of the Spivey girls drove their father's Ford sedan up to the fence of the cemetery and parked. They introduced Lois to the dozen young people already there, making a point of saying that Lois had come from Houston for a few months to help her grandmother, Missus Satchleben. The girls stood on one side of the fire while the boys stood opposite and talked among themselves. Cars and trucks arrived. A few boys rode up on horses and tied the reins to the cemetery fence.

Standing between the Spivey girls, Lois stole glances through the fire at some of the boys. One boy in particular caught her eye when he drove up to the church and parked his dark green truck. It was an old Ford, from before the war, with large front and rear fenders and a dusty hue to the paint. But it was in good shape and newly washed. The boy parked at the side of the church and waited a few minutes before getting out and walking toward the group gathered around the fire. Lois wanted to know who he was, but didn't know the others well enough to ask about him. She had no idea what designs the other girls might have on him. As he reached the fire, Lois saw him pull down the untucked tail of his shirt and force his shoulders back.

He was almost six and a half feet tall, his strong shoulders slightly stooped. He wore dungarees, a square-tailed short-sleeved plaid shirt, and Brogan boots. His hair was cut in a flat top that set off his handsome square face. Everything about him seemed new, even his boots. His hair looked like it had been cut that day. Lois thought that he looked like a man just released from prison. Although everyone there seemed to know him, he appeared cautious, as if he didn't spend much time with large groups of people. The girls all said hello as he approached the fire, and he shook hands with the boys. He was perhaps as young as fifteen or as old as twenty. Lois couldn't tell.

Although she had never dated a boy like him, she had seen them before, mostly when she was in the country. Boys who sat on the curbs outside feed stores or at the gates to saw mills, their lanky limbs folded in on themselves. Their hungry faces followed everyone who passed by. She saw them working at service stations, walking out to pump gas, wiping grease from their hands with blood-red rags. They always looked at her with a mixed expression of desire and hatred. Lois met their stares with fear and attraction. She felt superior to them. She knew these kinds of boys were trouble, her mother had warned her, but she was drawn to them like a fly to shit.

What Lois saw in these boys she could never find on the faces of the older country men. She wondered what happened to these boys when they grew up, what kind of men they became.

The boy shifted back and forth between his feet. Lois could sense he didn't want to be there. He stood directly across the fire from her. She met his eyes every time she looked up. He nodded to acknowledge her.

Lois didn't want to be there either.

When the Spivey girls walked away from the fire to get soft drinks, the boy walked to Lois's side.

"Hi. I'm Carlos." He stuck out his hand.

They shook hands. "I'm Lois."

"Nice to meet you."

"You too."

"You just move in around here somewhere?"

"No, I'm just staying with my grandparents. Do you know the Satchlebens?"

"You mean old Mister Otto? The German?"

"Yes."

The boy moved closer to Lois and they both looked into the fire. "I've been coon hunting with him. Does he still have that good red tick bitch?"

"I don't know. He has a bunch of dogs."

"I'd sure like to get a puppy out of that dog." Carlos looked at the young men and women standing around the fire. "You know many of these folks?"

"Just a couple. The Spivey girls. That's who brought me." Lois turned toward Carlos and moved slightly closer to him. "You still in school?"

"No, Daddy made me quit after sixth grade to help in the fields. I would've finished next year, though. You in school?"

"No, I graduated over a year ago."

"Where'd you go to school at?"

"Beaumont. French High School in Beaumont."

"The big city."

"Yeah, I guess it is compared to here."

They stood and watched the sparks from the hot pine fire float up from the flames.

"Did you hear the Texas City explosion where you was at?"

"What?"

"When Texas City exploded a few years back. Where were you? Did you hear it, or feel it?"

"Oh, yeah. We were living in Port Arthur at the time. The whole house shook and the windows even rattled. Momma thought it was the end of the world."

"We was plowing on the Hart place and we didn't know what had happened. It sounded like thunder and we could feel it in the ground too. More than a hundred and seventy-five miles away and we could feel and hear it. Daddy wouldn't let Momma go to the house to listen on the radio for news, so we didn't know what it was until that night. It sure did kill a bunch of people, didn't it?"

"Yeah, it did."

Carlos pitched his empty Nehi bottle across the fire and into a trash barrel. "I think I'm gonna be leaving out in a minute. You need a ride home?"

"I guess not, the Spiveys can take me back with them."

"Well, I guess what I meant to ask was, do you want a ride home with me?"

Lois sat against the passenger door as he drove down the single lane dirt road toward her grandparents' house. The bushes on the sides of the road reached across the shallow ditches and at times touched the side of the truck. The dim headlights of his pickup truck cast a gray hue onto the leaves that in daylight were brilliant green. A pale yellow glow from the dashboard illuminated Carlos's forearms. Lois couldn't read his face. She moved her pocketbook from her lap to the seat between them.

Carlos drove past the turnoff to her grandparents' place.

"That's the way home."

"I know, but I want to show you something. A surprise." He turned his head to look at her and smiled.

She crossed her ankles and looked ahead.

He slowed. The truck's axles bumped as they crossed a ditch and turned down a narrower road into the woods. "I hope it's still down there. The Boatmans are in here cutting some timber for Mister Langston and they might have tore it all down."

At a small opening in the woods Carlos stopped the truck. The headlights of the truck lit a roughly constructed lot made from saplings and rusted barbed wire. Two large mules stood side by side in the lot, their eyes silver disks in the headlight beams.

"Thems the mules Mister Boatman uses to skid the logs. He just leaves them here to save having to move them back and forth between his place and the woods. They cut down the logs and trim em, then they use the mules to skid the logs through the woods to this clearing. When they have a load bunched, they use the mules to work the loader to haul the logs up on the truck. Then while Mister Boatman is gone to the sawmill with the load, his niggers work cutting and bunching another load."

Lois heard pride in Carlos's voice as he explained this to her. It seemed important to him, knowing country things that he could explain to her, a girl from the city.

He turned off the headlights and they sat in darkness. Lois looked across the cab and could see the faintest outline of his profile, the shape of his forearm only two feet away.

"Let's give our eyes a few minutes to adjust before we try to get out. Since I don't smell it, though, I don't think it's still here. But we can go take a look."

Carlos opened the door and stepped out of the truck. Lois saw that there was even a little moonlight. When she stepped out of the truck, the heels of her shoes sank in the sand of the clearing. Her eyes became accustomed to the darkness. Carlos stood at the front of the truck with his hand on the hood.

"If it's still there, it starts just over that ridge." Carlos pointed to a line of trees at the edge of the clearing and began to walk. Lois followed.

As they reached the trees, Lois felt a breeze traveling up from the bottom of the hill on which they stood. It carried a fragrance as sweet as any perfume, fresh and clean. Carlos walked to her side. "It's wisteria. About an acre of it. It's even stronger down the hill, under the vines. If the wind is just right, you can even smell it all the way to the road sometimes. I found it when I was squirrel hunting back in here."

He closed his eyes and took a deep breath. Lois watched as his chest rose under his shirt, his shoulders moved back and his chin lifted. She thought this place and his love for it must be a secret he would be embarrassed to share with anyone who knew him.

Lois took a deep breath and stared up at his face. His eyes were still closed. She extended the fingers of her left hand and touched his arm between his shoulder and elbow.

A shiver traveled the length of his body. Lois couldn't tell if he had felt her touch. He turned to look at her. "My momma always says when you shake like that, a rabbit just run over your grave."

Lois smiled.

His hand reached back for hers and they walked down the hill together.

They were under the canopy of wisteria before Lois realized it. She expected to see the ground covered with small bushes like the ones she saw in gardens in Beaumont or Houston. But this was wild wisteria. Vines as thick as Lois's arm covered the trunks of the pine trees, crossed from the lower limbs and extended to the very tops of the trees. Looking up into the moonlit sky, Lois could see clumps of blooms hanging overhead, like bunches of grapes. Beyond the vines, she could see the clouds passing under the moon.

Carlos moved his hand to her waist. "Let's sit down."

"I don't want to mess up my dress."

"It's okay, the ground is covered with pine straw. See?"

He picked up a handful of straw and held it in front of her face. She took it from him, brought the straw close to her nose and took a deep breath.

He sat down at her feet, his hand lightly tracing the pleats of her skirt from her waistband to the hem. He patted the ground at his side.

Lois sat, careful to keep her knees and ankles together and to cover her legs with her skirt. Carlos lay back next to her, his fingers laced behind his head. "Look up."

She lowered her back to the ground and looked up at the sky beyond the trees. She shifted her focus between the moon and clouds and the pine tree branches with the vines. She felt dizzy and closed her eyes. She took another deep breath of the sweet wisteria.

She felt his hand on her stomach.

Without saying a word, he moved his hand up the fabric of her belt and touched her breast. His fingers were stiff and there was tension in his touch.

With his free hand he slowly unbuckled his belt, opened his fly, and pulled his dungarees down to his thighs. He reached beneath the hem of Lois's skirt and lifted it above her waist, then pulled her panties down and over one shoe. He left them around one ankle.

She recalled what her mother and the preacher had told her, but she couldn't see the evil in what they were doing and she couldn't sense the devil in this boy or in her. She didn't want to say no and was afraid that saying anything might make him stop.

He rolled over on top of her. She wanted to kiss him, but he buried his face at the nape of her neck. With his forearms under her arms and his hand on the top of her shoulders, he pulled her body down as he thrust upward. As he entered her, she moved her face to see him, but he shifted to avoid her gaze. He lifted her legs with his thighs and began to push inside her. Her right shoe fell from her foot.

He stopped and sat up, his weight on his knees. He took his shirt off and tossed it aside. His chest was white as baby's skin. He then lowered himself back on top of her, and she breathed and felt as if her body was expanding to cover the ground around her. Her shoulders touched the soft straw beneath her. Her relaxation was met by a growing urgency in his body. His sharp hip bones pressed against her thighs.

She wrapped her arms around his back and held him tight. The sinews of his back flexed with each thrust. His knees were locked and his weight now rested on the tips of his Brogan boots. She thought of a newsreel she had seen of soldiers doing pushups. His breath was quick and he dug his chin into her shoulder. A shudder passed through his body as he came inside her.

He relaxed his legs and settled down on top of her. She shifted beneath him and felt moisture on her neck and shoulder. She looked at his face. Tears streamed down his cheeks and gathered at the point of his chin.

When he saw her looking at him he jumped to his feet, pulled up his underwear and dungarees, and buckled his belt.

Lois sat up and lowered her skirt over her knees. It was wet with perspiration, and wrinkled. He turned his back to her. "Are you okay?" He did not respond. "Carlos, are you okay?"

"I'm fine. Let's go."

He spoke without turning and walked back up the hill toward the truck.

They rode in silence to her grandparents' house.

August 1950

Lois sat in a rocking chair on the front porch when Carlos's pickup came down the road toward her grandparents' house, a cloud of dust behind it. She hadn't seen him since the night they met, but she recognized the truck. He turned into their yard and parked under the cedar tree at the side of the house. Lois walked to the steps and hushed the dogs that came from under the house to bark. Carlos rolled down the window and leaned his head out.

"Mister Lawson at the mill said Mister Otto needed to see me about something. He said it was about a coon dog."

Lois walked down the steps and stood next to the fender of the truck. Carlos rested his arm on the window frame and adjusted the mirror. "No, I told Papa to leave word for you."

"Oh."

"Yeah, we need to talk about something."

"About what?"

Lois put her hand on the chrome handle of the door of the truck. "Can you get out for a minute?"

"Them dogs okay?"

"They won't bite. They just don't know you."

Lois walked to a bench beside the cedar tree and sat down.

Carlos moved to the front of his truck and leaned back against the grill, his arms across his chest.

"So, what do we need to talk about?"

Lois put her hands on her knees and looked down at them. She lowered her voice.

"I'm P. G."

"What does that mean? You mad at me about something?"

"No, it means I'm, we're, going to have a baby. I'm pregnant. P. G."

"What?"

Carlos shook his head, stood up straight and walked back to the side of the truck. He looked around the yard and at the front door of the house.

"And what makes you think I had anything to do with that?"

"Carlos, I haven't been with anybody else and I've been here all summer. You have to be the daddy."

Lois stood and walked toward him. He took a step back, his hands in front of him.

"I see what you're trying to do. It's clear to me. You were dressed up like a whore that night. I know what you were trying to do. You came up here to try and find a hardworking man like me to marry, probably ran out of men down there in Houston, or your reputation was so bad you knew you couldn't find a man, or at least one that would marry you. I know how you city girls are. I've heard how people talk about your people around here. German. How your own momma's nothing but a whore. How many times has she been married?"

Carlos got into his truck and slammed the door.

"Carlos, wait. We have to talk about this. About what we're gonna do."

"*We* don't have to do nothing. You need to go back where you come from. I won't have anything to do with this or you. I'm not gonna get trapped by you. It ain't mine."

He started his truck, backed into the road, and spun the tires as he drove away.

Lois ran up the steps and into the house. The screen door slammed as she disappeared down the hallway.

August 1950

Lois sat in a chair, her dress sweaty from her walk from the bus station. Her suitcase rested just inside the front door. Her mother and Mister Hughes sat on the sofa across from her.

"Momma, I need to talk to you about something."

"No!"

She had not even said the words, yet her mother knew what she had come to tell them. Lois nodded. She was relieved that she wouldn't have to say the actual words.

"Didn't I warn you? Didn't I tell you this could happen? This is the devil's doin. I thought you'd be safer up there with Momma and Daddy than down here. I sent you up there to keep you out of trouble, not to cause it. Now look what you've done. I didn't raise no sinner or a whore."

Lois, clinched hands in her lap, looked down at her knees. A roar filled her ears and blunted the edge of her mother's voice.

Mister Hughes looked at her mother and shook his head. He and her mother exchanged a glance. "Mister Hughes is right. Don't think we're gonna give you a place to have a bastard baby. What about the daddy? Who is he? Do you even know?"

"Probably one of those trashy no-count boys up there in the

country. Some hick. Or a nigger. I wouldn't even put that past her now."

Her mother moved to the end of the sofa and looked away from Lois.

"You are not my daughter. I raised you right. I raised you in the church. No daughter of mine would be in this kind of trouble."

"But Momma, you were—"

Her mother jumped to her feet and raised her hand across her chest, as if ready to backhand her daughter. "Don't you but Momma me. And don't you think you can cast a single stone. And don't think you can run back up to your grandparents and think they'll take care of you. You know they can barely take care of themselves, not to mention you and a bastard baby."

Mister Hughes took a step toward her. "Stop looking down like that. You look at your momma when she's talking to you."

"And don't think your brothers will take you in either. I'll see to that. You've made your bed, now you can just lay in it."

Mister Hughes stood in front of her. "The daddy wouldn't have you either, would he? I don't blame him. He got what he wanted, didn't he? Spoiled goods, easy, a whore. That's what he thought you were and you proved him right."

"I won't have nobody at church finding out about this either. I tell you what, you can just pick up that suitcase young lady and walk back out."

Lois turned her head as if slapped.

"Girl, you better listen to your momma and git."

Her mother rushed by her, ran down the hallway and slammed the bathroom door behind her. Mister Hughes walked into the hallway and picked up her suitcase.

"Momma?" Her mother didn't answer.

"You better git on out of here girl. You heard your momma."

"Momma!" Lois screamed, her face wet with tears.

Mister Hughes walked to the front door and held it open. Lois looked down the hallway where her mother had disappeared.

"Girl, you better git." He held the suitcase out to her.

She went to the door, took her bag from him, and walked back out into the heat.

August 1950

Fusako knew Weldon was dead when she looked up from her desk and saw Captain Harvey walk through the door at the end of the hallway. His hat was in his left hand and a piece of yellow paper was in his right. And Captain Harvey saw it in her face because as he walked the length of the hall he shook his head slowly, so that his words were useless when he arrived at her desk.

"No, no, no, no."

She kept the rhythm of her cries with her fists against the top of the desk.

Captain Harvey threw his hat onto one of the empty waiting room chairs. He walked around the side of the desk and embraced her. She tried to lash out with her hands. He held her wrists together and brought them to his chest.

"Fusako, Fusako. I'm sorry."

"No. No. No. Don't say it. Not true." As her voice returned she thrashed within his arms. "A mistake. It can't be true. Captain Harvey, you know the Army. They make many mistakes."

"No, Fusako. I spoke with Weldon's commanding officer myself. He was killed on the 7th of August. I have the confirmation here, if you want to see it."

He held out the yellow paper: *Second Lieutenant. David Weldon Scogin. 7 August 1950. Killed in action by hostile fire. Service number: 2212012*

Three nights. They spent three nights together as husband and wife before he was sent away to Korea.

On their wedding night, they lay side by side in her bed at Doctor Ito's house. She wore a silk nightgown that tied at her neck and hung to just below her knees. He wore a white military undershirt and dark green boxer shorts. He leaned back against the wall behind the bed and she lay at his side, tucked under his arm with her head resting on his chest. He talked without end, as if he had been saving some stories to tell her once they were man and wife. He talked of women and war.

He told her about the other Japanese girls before her, how his buddies laughed at him for refusing to go with them. He said when he looked at their faces, into those dark sad eyes, he couldn't go to bed with them. He had gone to the brothels with his buddies, and taken rations and candy and cigarettes with him, but he just gave the things to the girls and walked away.

Then he had found her. He said the sadness he saw behind her eyes was different. Her eyes told of what was lost when those of the other girls told of what had been given away. Those sad eyes in that pretty face. He said they were enough to break a grown man's heart.

He told her about fighting in the war. How he had started in North Africa then moved to Sicily, on to Naples and Anzio, then finally all the way into Germany. He told of the buddies he lost, of the death he had seen. He told her about being trapped in a basement of a house for six days, surrounded by German snipers, while the body of one of his buddies rotted in the street in front of the house. He told her of the dog that came each day for a ration of his buddy's flesh. He couldn't shoot the dog or retrieve his buddy's body out of fear of drawing the German fire.

He cried and Fusako held him tight, her arm across his chest and her head tucked under his chin. She felt his tears as they soaked into her hair, running down his cheeks and chin and onto the top of her head.

They woke in the morning in the same position, still clothed. Weldon returned to his base without knowing when he would be able to spend the next night with his wife.

One month later, on their second night together, they made love. When they were finished, Fusako rested her cheek on Weldon's bare chest and looked down the length of his naked body to his thin white feet at the end of the bed. She felt so small next to him. Her feet touched his shins just beneath his knees. He talked and she felt the vibration of his voice through his chest.

"Fusako, we can run off together. We both have a lot to run from. Just the two of us. As soon as I'm done in Korea, we'll go back to the States and make our own life together. I can get a good job and we can forget our families and what happened to us, the war and all. We can live just the way we want, just the two of us." Weldon brought his hands together, as if in prayer. She looked beyond his hands to the lamp on the table in the corner of the room. She closed her eyes against the brilliance of the light.

Another flash of light. Her brothers. Her parents. Now Weldon. All gone. Was it her fault? What had she done to deserve such loss? Were the people of the town correct? A dark fist held her tight, forced the breath from her lungs. The bomb. Dr. Ito. The walk. Her work. Weldon. Now nothing. Another bomb. No escape. She was now trapped.

After their marriage she had felt pursued, as if a mob of her own people might arrive at the door to her house and pull her into the street, shave her head. Knowing that she had Weldon allowed her to ignore the stares on the street as she walked from Dr. Ito's house to his office to work. She was already a stranger in her own country and now he was gone and she had no escape. Knowing that she was leaving, knowing that she had a place with him, away from her country, had allowed her to survive.

The third and final night they spent together, they spoke of their future. He had promised her that he was done with fighting. She could still hear the echo of his words from less than a month before.

"My buddy from the Army in Europe has found me and him jobs at a plant in Orange, Texas. My C.O. says that as soon as this trouble is over in Korea they will let me be discharged. My time will be up and we can leave. We will be in Texas within six months at the most."

"But danger there. Korea. You could get hurt?"

"But Sugar, I don't have any choice. The damned North Koreans have invaded the South and I'm being sent there. We're the closest forces they have, so we are the ones going. That's all there is to it."

"But you are almost finished. We move to Orange soon, no?"

"Yes, but I have to do this first. I won't be gone long. I promise."

Her sobs faded. She leaned against the back of the sofa on which she and Captain Harvey sat. Her tears had left a stain on the front of his starched uniform shirt.

"Fusako, there is one more thing. The Army did make one mistake. Weldon's file still said he was unmarried, so they have already shipped his body back to his family in Texas. There is nothing we can do about that now. I tried. Do you have his family's address in the States? I can help you write to them to see what they can do to help you."

September 1950

Mildred stood on the top porch step with her head cocked to hear if Carlos was still in the barn hitching the mules or if he had already left for the field. She heard the jangle of the trace chains from inside the barn. He hadn't left yet. Her son had already been in the field almost an hour but she thought she might have a chance to make the beds before she had to follow her own team into the field. At least her son had hitched her mules for her.

As she turned to go back inside the house Mildred looked down the long lane that led from their house out to the main road. She recognized the pickup truck of Robert Higgenbotham, their mail carrier, driving up the lane toward her. The only time Mildred could recall that Mr. Higgenbotham had ever driven up the lane to the house was the time that he brought the box with the .22 rifle Carlos had ordered for their son from Sears and Roebuck. The long package wouldn't fit in the wooden box nailed to the corner fence post down by the road where he usually left their mail, and he had known Carlos would raise hell with the postmaster if he had to wait until his next trip to town to pick up the rifle.

And Mildred was sure they hadn't ordered anything from Sears and Roebuck. She stood on the porch and watched as the black Ford pickup made its way up the lane. Mister Higgenbotham didn't look at her as he came to a stop in front of the steps.

"Morning, Missus Dews. Is Carlos around the house anywhere?"

"Now Mister Higgenbotham, you know to call me Mildred."

Mister Higgenbotham was the thinnest man Mildred had ever known. People in town always said it was a good thing he had that post office job because he didn't look strong enough to do any other kind of work.

"Well, Mildred, then you better call me Bob."

"I think we have a deal, then."

As he stepped out of the truck, the mail carrier tucked a letter into the breast pocket of his shirt. Mildred walked to the side of the truck and shook his hand. "He's out in the barn. I just heard him hitching up Fuzzy and Blue. You sure are early today with that mail."

"Yes, Mam, I've got something I need to talk to Carlos about."

"Well, don't keep him long. He is on a tear this morning. You know how he is."

"I do, Mildred. But this is important." He turned and walked to the barn, closing the small door cut into the larger door after stepping inside. Mildred walked back in the screen door to finish washing the breakfast dishes. She hoped she still had time to make the beds before she went out to the field.

As she rinsed the last of the plates, Mildred heard two sets of footsteps come up the steps and onto the front porch. "Mildred, come on out here," Carlos yelled out. "Me and Mister Higgenbotham need to show you something."

She walked to the front of the house, drying her hands on a dish towel. The two men stood on the porch facing the door and watched as Mildred walked up the center hallway toward them. Mister Higgenbotham held a letter in his hand.

"Mildred, now don't go getting all upset or something, but the post office done got this letter back that you wrote to your brother. It's got a stamp on it that's gonna upset you."

Mildred flicked the dish towel over her right shoulder and opened the door. The frame of the screen hit Carlos's boot and stopped. She reached through the crack in the door and took the letter from Mister Higgenbotham's hand.

Mildred recognized her own handwriting and the envelope she used whenever she wrote to Brother. She even knew which letter it was: the first she had written to him since he had gone over from Japan to Korea. She had written to him throughout the war in Europe, but only learned later exactly where he had been. She knew, just like he wrote in his letters, that he was somewhere in North Africa, somewhere in Italy, then finally, somewhere in Germany. Mildred couldn't believe that he chose, after the war was over, to stay in the Army. After all that fighting and killing he had seen and done in Africa and Europe, she couldn't believe he was going halfway around the world in the other direction to Japan. He said he would be safe over there, that he was part of the Occupation Forces, not fighting anymore. Then when the fighting started in Korea they had sent him over there. She had learned a new military address for him each time he was transferred.

A stamp of muddy red ink covered part of his address.

War Department. Recipient Deceased. Return to Sender.

She dropped to her knees then collapsed onto her back, the letter folded in her grip. She saw the letter in her fist, creased by her clamped fingers. She wanted to open her hand and see the ink of the stamp gone from the envelope. But it was still there.

Carlos and Mister Higgenbotham rushed in the door. "Now Sugar, don't go getting all tore up. You know how the Army is. Somebody somewhere just messed something up." Carlos reached down and lifted Mildred to her feet. Mister Higgenbotham brought in a chair from the kitchen. She sat down. "Sugar, we don't know nothin for sure. Mister Higgenbotham says that the postmaster has done sent a telegram to the Army in Washington to try to find out something."

Mister Higgenbotham squatted beside her. "And your daddy got a letter from your brother just yesterday. So how could that be?"

Ignoring the two men, Mildred stood, walked across the porch and sat on the top step, pulling the fabric of her cotton dress over her legs and drawing her knees up to her chin. She wouldn't move until she knew for sure.

Mister Higgenbotham left, promising to let them know if he found out anything from Washington. When Carlos or their boy approached her during the day Mildred wouldn't say a word and simply swiped her hands at them and rested her forehead back on her knees. In the afternoon, when the sun crossed over the top of the house and began to shine in Mildred's face, Carlos tried to convince her to come inside, but she wouldn't move. And when her son came in from the field at the end of the day, she had him sit next to her on the step. She said she wasn't gonna move until she knew for sure, one way or the other.

After the shadow from the barn in front of the house traveled across the yard and began to shade her, Mildred heard a car coming down the road from over by the Deloney place. She looked down the lane and waited to see if the car would turn up their drive. It did. She recognized the car. It was her sister Audrey and her husband Henry.

Mildred stood as the car came into the yard. Before it stopped, Audrey opened the car's door and jumped out. Mildred knew from the look on Audrey's face that the stamp on the letter had been correct. Their brother was dead. Brother was dead. And with that new wife over in Japan. Audrey held a telegram in her hand as she threw herself into Mildred's arms.

September 1950

"Lois? Excuse me. Are you Lois?"

The small woman called her name as Lois stepped out of the five and dime store at the end of her shift. Carrying a shopping bag with twine handles, the woman walked toward her. "Are you Lois Minter? Mister Otto Satchleben's granddaughter?"

Lois stepped back from the woman. "Yes, Mam, I am."

"I'm Mildred Dews, Carlos's momma."

"Oh."

Mildred looked at the people passing them on the sidewalk.

"Honey, can we go somewhere and talk?"

"Yes, Mam, I guess so. I was just on my way home from work. I've only got a little time before I have to be to work at my other job."

"That's okay, honey, I don't need too much of your time. Is there a café where we could get a cup of coffee and sit and talk?"

"Yes, Mam, there is one just down the street on the next corner."

They walked to the café in silence. Mildred asked for a booth in a corner. Mildred put the bag on the inside of the seat of the booth and sat down next to it. Lois sat across the booth from her. They both ordered coffee from the waitress. Mildred put her elbows on the table and lowered her hands across it to touch Lois's wrists.

"You are just the prettiest thing."

"Thank you, Mam."

"I know you don't know me from Adam's off ox, but I heard from your grandmomma how my boy treated you and I'm here to say I'm sorry. I wanna see what we can do."

Lois looked around the café at the small groups of diners in the other booths. The waitress brought their coffee and both women watched her walk away. "That's okay. I'm fine. You don't need to say anything."

"I've tried to raise Carlos better than that, and I'm gonna make sure we do the right thing for you. You just have to trust me and wait. I can't do anything right now, but I'll figure something out. You just need to sit tight and wait."

"I'm fine." Lois took a sip after adding sugar and cream to her coffee.

"Your grandmother told me you were living by yourself and working two jobs. That ain't fine to me. And what are you supposed to do when the time comes? You can't work all that time."

"My family will take care of me."

"Now Lois, your grandmomma told me about your momma and your stepdaddy. I know they ain't gonna help you none, and I know your momma won't let your grandparents have anything to do with you."

Lois looked down into her cup of coffee.

"I know this won't be no excuse for how he treated you, but it might help explain how my boy behaved. I just want you to listen. You don't have to say a thing, honey. I mean it. Just sit there and listen."

Mildred leaned over the table toward Lois.

"I've been married to my Carlos Dews for twenty years now, and I've been the mother of another Carlos Dews for sixteen years. I've tried all those years to figure out how to live with them and love them, and I think it would help you to know a few of these things. Now I've studied Carlos, my husband, trying to figure out why he is the way he is, why he is so damned mean and hateful and why he seems to be determined to make our boy as much like him as he can.

"It started with his daddy's daddy and it's been passed on from daddy to daddy to daddy. I think they feel that something's wrong with them, and the only way to hide it is to work as hard as they can every day. And they are just as hard on themselves as they are on everybody else.

"A woman shouldn't say something like this about her own boy, but you don't want to be with my boy. You don't want him to marry you. He already has too much of his daddy in him. I've tried but failed in changing my husband and keeping him from making our boy in his image. I've had about enough. I'm trying to find a way out for us all.

"I can't be hopeful about how my boy is going to behave and treat you and that baby you are carrying, but I can assure you, I will do whatever it takes to make sure you and that baby are taken care of. I had to hurt a baby once, and I swore to myself that I'd make sure that no baby was ever in that position again. I won't let us get into that shape with your little one.

"Don't get me wrong; my husband can be a mean son of a bitch, but he is the most tender-hearted man I've ever known. I've seen that man beat a dog bloody when it killed a chicken in the yard, and all the same I've seen him cry like a baby when one of his calves died, or if he sees that afflicted Thomas boy without any legs who hangs around in the town square scooting around on that cart he has, pushing himself around with his knuckles. More than once Carlos has come home from town and just cried like a baby over that Thomas boy.

"And now my boy is just like his daddy. I've never known any men like them before. It's like they can't help themselves from being tenderhearted and feeling things, but the minute they realize it, they have to do something hateful or mean to balance out their feeling something. My own papa is a mean son of a bitch, but he's that way all the time. He says he don't need anybody and means it. But these Dews men are different. They are tenderhearted. They'd never admit it but they cry at almost anything. They need lots of loving.

"I've caught Carlos with other women so many times. But I
stayed with him. I always just stayed with him. He's like a big old
baby. Each and every time he has begged me to forgive him and take
him back. Got down on his knees and cried and begged for me to
forgive him. Said he didn't know why he did it and promised not to
do it again. You just can't walk away and leave him on his own. He
just needs too much. It would be a sin to leave somebody who needs
that much from you. But I wouldn't want any other woman to find
herself in my position, either."

"Miss Mildred, I don't know what to say. I'm doing what I can."

"Well, let's talk about this baby. I've only had one baby that lived
because I almost died having Carlos. He just tore me up inside. If
it wasn't for my Aunt Neva we would have both died. That's why I
don't want you to do anything against this baby. Don't give it away,
and surely don't do anything to hurt it. I know how precious a baby
can be. Don't do anything to this baby. Just wait. Just because its
daddy hurt you so bad don't mean you need to take it out on the in-
nocent baby. You don't know, honey. This baby could make all the
difference in the world. Just because it's from its daddy don't mean it
has to be like its daddy. We can make it different.

"My own momma had eleven babies but only seven of us lived.
I'm the oldest. And she died having my littlest brother. And he died
too. When I try to remember my own momma, all I can see in my
mind is her either crying or pregnant or both. But I remember her
telling me when she was pregnant with the last baby that lived, my
brother Beamon, that she wouldn't trade one of her babies for all
the happiness in the world.

"I don't know if you heard about it, but I just lost my brother
in Korea. Weldon. He was the oldest of the brothers. And now I'm
fighting to get his wife over here from Japan. He was in Japan at the
end of the war and married this Jap girl. I've gotta get that girl over
here from Japan. But since the war, they're not letting no Japs into
the country. She is the only thing I got left from my brother. That's
what we called him since he was the oldest boy, Brother. I'm telling
you all this so you know that I know what I'm talking about. I've

been there. I promise that as soon as I get that taken care of I will figure out something for you and the baby. Just wait.

"You should have seen how my husband Carlos was when I first heard that Brother had been killed over in Korea. He was just the best behaving man you ever saw. Petting me and taking care of me like he didn't have a mean bone in his body. But I know that there will be meanness coming in the future, to make up for all that loving and petting. And I bet Carlos was just the same with you. Nice at first, tender, then mean to make up for it.

"I know all of this don't make any sense. And I'll probably burn in hell for having talked about my boy the way I have, but I just want you to know that there's a story behind why Carlos has done what he did to you, and that I aim to do what is right by you and that baby you are carrying. He already has too much of his daddy in him. I don't want you to do nothing to hurt this baby. Don't do nothing to hurt that baby just because my boy didn't treat you right. Don't do nothing to that baby out of spite. Babies are precious."

Outside the coffee shop, Mildred reached inside her bag and pulled out a bundle wrapped in brown paper and tied with baling twine. She gave it to Lois.

"I'll get you out of here, one way or another. I'll do what's right by you and this baby. Just wait. That's all I ask. Just wait. This baby could make all the difference in the world. It could make all the difference in the world."

Lois walked into her room and put the bundle on the table. She went to the dresser and removed her only knife, moved the package to the middle of the table and cut the twine where it formed a cross. She knew what it was as soon as she opened the brown paper. A baby quilt in the Dutch doll pattern, just like the ones she saw at her grandparents' house. She lifted it to her nose and smelled the fresh, clean cotton and a mixture of corn and flour from the sacks that had been used to piece it.

Something fell to the table from inside the quilt. A bundle of money, tied with the same twine. She untied the bow at the center of the bills and counted ones, fives, tens, and twenties. Written in a perfect hand, in dark pencil, next to the portrait on each bill were two words. *Just wait.*

Three hundred dollars. More money than Lois had ever seen before. But still not enough.

October 1950

L ois stood at the bottom of the stairs that led to the garage apart- ment. She wanted to catch her breath before walking up but was afraid someone might see her if she lingered there too long. She wouldn't know what to say. She didn't even know the man's name. Just directions to where he lived, or at least where he did it, and the name of a girl at work who had been there. "The garage apartment down by the rail yards, at the back of a lot with old cars next to the Esso station." As she walked, she repeated the directions until they sounded like an awkward poem.

After finding the place, she had walked up and down the block three times just to see what it looked like, how a place where some- one *did that* looked. She felt like she did when she walked by a honky- tonk, or a house where she knew whores lived.

She wondered what he would do. She hadn't had the nerve to ask that. Would he cut her somewhere, or put a needle into her stomach? Would he touch her down there or was it done from the outside? Was it some kind of pill? Would she bleed? What would he do it with? Would she have to look at it? Would she be awake or asleep? Would she have to stay there or could she leave when he was done?

It had taken all her strength and three weeks of trying to ask where she could find someone like him. And now all she had to do was climb the stairs.

Lois stood on the landing at the top of the stairs and knocked on the door. Its four panes of glass rattled in their frame. Footsteps inside vibrated the floorboards under her feet. The red face of a man appeared in the parted curtains of the door then disappeared. She felt more hurried footsteps inside.

The man opened the door, buttoning a sweat-stained shirt. "Howdy. What can I do you for?"

"I'm a friend of Diane. She works at McCrory's. She told me to come see you about something. She said you would know her and what it's about."

"Okay then. Come on in."

She walked past him into the apartment. He walked out on the landing in his bare feet and looked around before following her inside and closing the door.

Along one wall of the small apartment was a counter with a tiny sink, with a hotplate at its side. A rusty refrigerator stood at the end of the counter. A round table and two chairs were in the center of the room. A red checked oilcloth covered the table. The floors were bare and sheets were tacked over all the windows. A twin bed, without pillows and covered with a white sheet, was pushed into a corner. An open door in another corner led to a small bathroom.

"Have a seat."

Holding her purse against her stomach, Lois walked to the table. They sat across from each other. He looked her up and down.

"You smell like popcorn."

"I make the popcorn at McCrory's."

"I need to ask you a couple of questions. What's your name?"

"Millie. What's yours?"

"You can call me Stan. Now, how *did* you find me here?"

"Diane at work told me she knew you."

"Oh yeah, Diane. She have long black hair and a mole on her cheek?"

"Yes, that's Diane."

"Did you come alone?"

"Yeah, I walked from work."

"Well, you can get Charlie down at the Esso to call you a taxicab when you leave."

Lois put her elbows on the table and rested her forehead in her hands.

"You okay?"

"I'm just a little light-headed and hot from the walk. Could I have a glass of water?"

"Sure thang."

He rinsed a glass from off the counter and filled it from the tap.

Lois looked at it and took a drink. The water tasted like rust.

"You been to a doctor?"

"Yes, but just when I first found out."

"What's his name? The doctor."

"Doctor Snyder. But he's up in Nacogdoches County, that's where I was when it happened."

"How far along are you?"

"Three or four months."

"I'm glad you didn't wait any more. You know, the earlier the better. It just makes it easier. But you don't have anything to worry about. I was almost a doctor. I had two years of medical school in Galveston and I work in a nursing home now. You want us to do it today?"

"How much would you need for it?"

"A hundred dollars. Cash. You got that with you?"

"Yeah, I do."

Lois opened her purse and put her hands inside. She looked down, counted out the bills inside the bag and put them on the table in front of her. He took the money, leaned back in his chair, and stuffed it into his pocket.

"You don't happen to have a sanitary napkin and a belt with you? I don't have any here. You'll need something because you might bleed some."

"No."

"That's okay. We'll rig up something with toilet paper and your underwear when we're done. You have to work tomorrow?"

"Yes. I have to work at both my jobs tomorrow."

"Well, you're gonna have to take a few days off and stay at home. It's better if you lay down mostly for a couple of days. Stay off your feet. If you have the weekends off, it might be better to do it this Friday when you get off work."

"I don't ever have two days in a row off and I want to do it now."

"Well we can do it now if you think you can tough it out at work tomorrow. But you come back here if you have any problems. Don't go to no doctor or to the hospital. If I'm not here, you can ask Charlie at the Esso to get in touch with me. He knows where to find me. You'll have some bleeding. That's normal. But if it gets bad you need to come back. I'll get it all today so you won't need to worry about anything solid passing. If there are any clumps or anything, those are just like scabs."

He stood and leaned against the refrigerator.

"What you need to do is go into the bathroom there and empty your bladder. Then take off your stockings and panties. When you're done, I'll go in to wash up a bit. While I'm in there, you can lay down on the bed with your butt near the end and your knees up. Lay on top of the sheet. Either take off your dress or pull it way up around your waist. Oh, and take off your shoes."

The bathroom smelled of mold. Lois tried to pee but couldn't. She sat on the toilet lid and removed her shoes. She took off her stockings and panties and stuffed them into her purse. She stood and looked at herself in the medicine cabinet mirror. She leaned in and looked into her eyes, resting her forehead against the mirror. The glass was cool, and the tip of her nose and chin pressed against the glass. She pushed her lips against the mirror and kissed her reflection. She closed her eyes, listened to her heartbeat and noticed every breath.

Pushing herself away from the sink, she wiped her eyes with the back of her hand. She stared at the red smear of lipstick on the mirror.

He knocked on the door. "Are you okay?"

"I'll be right out."

"Okay, take your time. I just wanted to be sure you was okay."

Lois walked out of the bathroom, holding her shoes in one hand, her purse in the other.

"I'll be right out. Just wait. Get ready like I said." He entered the bathroom and closed the door.

She went to the bed and sat down. The smell of rubbing alcohol now mingled with the stuffy air of the room. On a small table next to the bed there was a shallow dishpan, partially covered by a towel. She lifted the cloth and saw two glistening instruments submerged in the alcohol. One looked like a smooth silver pistol and the other like a teaspoon with a sharp edge and a long, long handle.

He was still in the bathroom. Water running. "Just wait."

Lois ran to the door, her purse and shoes clutched to her chest. She ran down the stairs and across the lot. She put on her panties, stockings, and shoes in the ladies' room of the Esso station then walked back to her rented room, the grit from the lot in front of his apartment still on the soles of her feet.

October 1950

Mildred's eyes returned to the spot where the tracks turned and disappeared southward. She sat sideways, her legs under her skirt hanging over the edge of the pickup seat and out the opened door. The truck was parked next to the train station in Nacogdoches. When they first arrived to wait for the midnight train that passed through Nacogdoches on its way between Houston and Texarkana, she had stared at the moonlight reflecting off the green ceramic roof tiles of the station. The slope of the roof, with the four corners kicked up just a bit, reminded her of the wedding pictures Brother had sent from Japan. Her brother and his new bride stood on the steps of a church, wearing embroidered silk robes, his black, hers white, or at least that is the way they looked in the photograph.

Carlos stood at the corner of the station next to the broad loading dock talking to the stationmaster, an old gray-haired man wearing a cap. Mildred thought he looked like a Yankee. The man told them he had stayed beyond his shift to help them, since the freight trains didn't usually stop at the passenger station.

PapaDavid and his new wife Lucille sat in their Buick sedan, looking straight ahead, only occasionally exchanging glances with one another as they talked. Mildred couldn't hear what they were saying because of the roar of the feed mill just down the tracks. But she didn't want to hear them anyway, or talk to them.

One of the hands from the mill walked up to her daddy's car. She watched as her father greeted him with a broad smile and a handshake; and she saw her father change his expression as he told the worker why they were waiting on the freight train in the middle of the night.

Mildred knew this was all an act. She would never forgive her father for his reaction to the government letter. How he had skipped a couple of steps to the news that he'd be getting money from his son's death. It was just like what she saw Hitler do in a newsreel during the war. A feeble rigid skip in response to good news, his body unable to contain his joy.

The steam whistle at the feed mill signaled midnight and the change of shift. Soon after, a flood of men, covered in dust from their work and carrying their tin lunch buckets, walked past on their way to the company houses along the tracks. Mildred knew it was time for the train to arrive, but she wanted it to be late tonight. She didn't want anyone other than the family to see them, to be there when Brother arrived on that train. In a box.

Mildred heard the wail of the train's whistle as it crossed the highway a few miles south of town. She again looked down the tracks, staring until she saw what she knew was the black and red engine of the Southern Pacific line make the bend, its bright headlight circling in its frame.

She remembered that as a child, lying in bed with Brother at her side, they could hear this very train from miles away as it passed between Nacogdoches and Garrison on its nightly trip from Houston to Texarkana and on to Chicago. As they shivered and drew nearer to one another, Brother always said the same thing: "That must be the lonesome-est sound in the world. That old train out there in the night, traveling all by itself. I know there are men in it, but it just seems to be crying out for somebody or something. It sounds like the end of the world to me."

The train pulled into the station. Mildred felt the heat from the engine as it passed her. The smell of diesel and hot iron made her recoil. The train let out another blast from its whistle. Mildred threw her hands against her ears; this close, the sound was like a man screaming in pain. She felt the rumble of the train in her body.

The stationmaster broke off his conversation with Carlos and walked up the tracks toward the engine. Mildred followed him with her eyes then looked at each car of the short train, wondering which one held her brother's coffin.

She stepped out of the pickup and walked to the edge of the platform. The station master returned with a man that climbed down the ladder on the side of the engine. The two men climbed the steps of the platform and walked to the broad wooden doors of one of the train's cars. With a loud clank, the man from the engine lifted the iron handle and slid the door open. Light poured out of the car onto the platform. Mildred saw what looked to be an office, lit by bulbs covered in wire cages that hung from the ceiling. There was a wide desk with a chair bolted to the floor in front of it. Shelves and cubby holes covered the walls, just like in the little post office in Garrison. Two men were inside. One wore a railroad uniform without the jacket and the other a soldier's uniform. The two men walked to the door and spoke to the stationmaster, who then turned and looked down from the platform into the darkness beyond it.

"Mister Scogin? I can't see you. If you are out there, could you come up here?"

Mildred turned to watch her father lean across the car seat and kiss his new wife before opening the car door and stepping out. He walked up the ramp at the end of the platform and joined the men in the door of the car. They all stepped inside and the door slid closed behind them.

Carlos walked to Mildred's side. "I wonder what they are doing in there. Since we're gonna miss at least a day's work with the funeral and all, day after tomorrow, I wanna be in the field early in the morning. I sure hope they finish up quick, whatever it is they are doing in there."

Carlos and Mildred stared at the slit of light at the door's edge.

It opened and Mildred's father stepped out. "Yawl all gather around here at the edge of the platform. They gonna be bringing him out here in a minute."

PapaDavid walked to the side of his car and opened the door for Lucille to join them. Carlos put his arm around Mildred's shoulders. The stationmaster and the man without his jacket walked out, each holding the leather strap at the end of a green wooden trunk.

Mildred gasped and brought her hands to her mouth. Carlos turned and looked down at her.

"Is that all that's left of him? In a trunk?"

The two men sat the trunk down at the edge of the platform. The stationmaster squatted in front of Lucille and PapaDavid. "Mister Scogin, Captain Fletcher in there says that this is all of your son's personal things. Everything he had with him in Korea when he was killed. He said it should have gone to his wife over there in Japan but for some reason they sent it with him."

With that, the stationmaster stood and walked back inside the car. Mildred expected to see a coffin when, a minute later, the four men came out onto the platform carrying a long narrow crate, two men at the ends and one on each side. They strained to lift its weight. The lid of the crate was held in place on all four sides by locks. They carried it to the edge of the platform, placed it alongside the trunk, walked down the ramp of the loading dock, lifted it onto their shoulders, then carried it to the back of Carlos and Mildred's pickup truck. The family followed the crate and watched as the men slid it into the bed of the truck. They loaded the trunk on top of the crate, just behind the rear window of the truck's cab.

The man from the railroad car shook Mister Scogin's hand then returned to his work in the train, closing the door behind him. The man from the engine walked back up the tracks and climbed the ladder back into the cab. The stationmaster, after speaking briefly to Mister Scogin, walked to his own car and drove away. Explaining that he would join them for the funeral in two days, Captain Fletcher walked to the end of the bed of the pickup, came to attention, saluted, then walked into the dark city in search of his hotel.

Mildred stood alongside the bed of the truck, her hand resting on the painted wood of the crate. She could hear Carlos and her father discussing how they'd unload the crate into the front room of the Scogin home.

"Carlos, you and Mildred can take that old trunk of his stuff on home with you. I'm sure there's nothing in there I need, or want."

As Mister Scogin turned to go, Carlos stopped him. "When they took you up in there before they brought him out, what was you doing? Signing some government papers or something?"

"No, they needed me to identify his remains, as they called them."

"You mean to say they had you look at him? After all this time?"

"Yes, they did. They opened that outer box, then the casket inside of it, and then opened up this sack they had him in."

"And could you tell it was him?"

"Yeah, I could. He was as black as any nigger you ever saw, but it was him for sure. I recognized my boy."

March 1951

A s soon as the pains began, Lois carried her suitcase and walked the four long blocks from her rented room to the hospital.

"Mam, what's your name?"

"Lois."

"Last name? Mam, your last name?"

"Shirers. Lois Shirers."

She lied. She used the maiden name of her sister-in-law.

"Husband's name?"

Lois looked down at the edge of the nurse's desk.

"Missus Shirers, what is your husband's name?"

Lois shook her head slowly.

"Oh. I see." Lois heard the nurse's pen scratch something onto the paper on the clipboard. "And what is your doctor's name?"

"I don't have one."

"You haven't seen a doctor during your pregnancy?"

"Just when I first found out."

"Is this your first child?"

"Yes."

"Do you have anybody with you?"

"No."

"What's the name of the father?"

Lois sat. Quiet.

"Miss Shirers, we must include the father's name. It must go on the certificate. You are required. If you are married within one year of the child's birth, the baby can have its daddy's last name. You'll just have to go to the courthouse."

"Okay. Dews. Carlos Dews. Carlos Weldon Dews. D-E-W-S. Dews."

March 1951

Mildred walked down the long drive toward the mailbox by the main road. She had heard Mister Higgenbotham's truck stop for just a few seconds and knew that he had left something in their tin mailbox. She had just enough time to walk down to the road and get whatever it was before Carlos was done sharpening the plow in the barn and would be ready for his dinner. When she opened the mailbox, she thought she had heard wrong and that Mister Higgenbotham hadn't stopped and put something in the box. As she began to close the rusty door of the mailbox she saw a postcard in the very back corner. She reached in and took it out.

The front of the postcard was covered with the word "Houston" in large letters on a red, white, and blue background. Each of the letters of the name was made up of small pictures of sites in and around the city. Mildred turned the card over. Next to her own simple address —Mildred Dews, Garrison, Texas—she found eleven words.

Baby boy.
All fine.
I named him Carlos.
Hotel Sam Houston.
L.

September 1951

Mildred knew the trip would be long. Almost two weeks to travel there and back. Five days of driving each direction, more than two days just to cross Texas, then New Mexico, Arizona, Nevada, and California, to Los Angeles then up that long coast all the way to San Francisco. Once there, they thought they would never find a hotel room. Actually never did. Mildred finally convinced a bellhop at the St. Francis Hotel to take pity on them and let them stay two nights in a room in the basement where the hotel staff sometimes took naps between shifts. The bellhop said there had been a housing shortage ever since the war, and now with the trouble in Korea even the hotels were all full. He said he had a buddy in the war from East Texas, so he had recognized Mildred's accent.

Mildred told this bellhop everything of their trip across the country, including how, when they stopped at a drive-in restaurant in Los Angeles, they saw a woman and a little girl in a convertible that she was sure was Lana Turner. And Mildred told him why they were there, of her brother dying over in Korea, of all the letters she had to write, of the congressman, a Mister Ralph Yarborough, who helped get a law passed just so her Japanese sister-in-law could come to live with them in East Texas. She told him how she had been interviewed by the FBI and had signed something called an affidavit saying that she would keep her sister-in-law under the same roof with her for at least two years or until she got married again. And she told him how they had come to meet the boat with her on it. It was to arrive the next morning.

She had the law memorized that the congressman had passed, just for her, and recited it to him. Private Law 516, Chapter 146. April 3, 1951. H.R. 5347. An Act. For the relief of Fusako Terao Scogin. Be it enacted by the Senate and House of Representatives of the United States of America in Congress assembled, That, notwithstanding the provisions of section 13 of the Immigration Act of 1924, as amended, Fusako Terao Scogin shall be held to be a non-quota immigrant and may be admitted to the United States for permanent residence if she is found to be otherwise admissible under the provisions of the immigration laws. Approved April 3, 1951.

Mildred, her younger sister Audrey, and their now oldest brother Wesley drove across the country in Wesley's brand-new Ford. Wesley had been out of Texas when he was overseas during the war, but Mildred and Audrey had never been outside the state, not even to Louisiana—only one county away from where they grew up. Wesley had a good job down in Orange that he got when he came back from the war. He had married his sweetheart OlaMae and they were doing fine down there in the city. He was the only one in the family with a car good enough to make the trip.

To get across the desert, they put a washtub in the front floorboard, put a big block of ice in it, and directed the car's vents to blow over it. They drank the cool water of the melted ice, cooled their faces with wash rags soaked in it, and rubbed pieces of ice chipped from the block on the backs of their necks.

They waited on the pier with a big crowd for their sister-in-law to walk down the gangplank. They watched as the giant ship pulled alongside the pier then inched its way closer, as big ropes were tied up. They listened to a brass band play as crowds of people streamed from the ship. They waited and waited, saw families reunited and baggage claimed. The crowds at the side of the ship thinned and the sun broke over the top of the ship. The line of people coming off the ship dwindled, then stopped. Men in suits began to walk up and down the gangplank. A man carrying a big camera came down off the ship and Mildred walked up to him.

"Mister, I'm so sorry to bother you, but me and my brother and sister here have come all the way across the country from Texas to meet our sister-in-law coming over from Japan. We looked at every person who came down off that boat and we didn't see her nowhere. Do you know who we could talk to and find out where she might be at?"

"Well, Mam, is your sister-in-law a Jap? Cause if she is, I think I just took her picture. There is all kinds of newspaper men up there interviewing her. It's something special since she is the first Jap to come into the country since the end of the war. You just wait right here, I'm sure they will bring her down here to you when they are done with her on the ship."

They waited another hour.

They had seen pictures of Fusako but they didn't realize just how small she was until she stepped from the deck of the ship onto the gangplank, a small suitcase in her right hand. When she stepped onto the pier Mildred ran to her and lifted her off the ground with a hug.

Two in the front seat and two in the back. After another night in their basement room at the hotel, they began the trip back across the country. When they got back to the desert, the washtub was put back in the front floorboard again and Audrey had to sit with her feet up under her the rest of the trip back. Four more days across the desert and Texas. They communicated with their sister-in-law using hand signals and the little English that Fusako knew.

Mildred talked during the entire trip from California to Texas. She thought that if she filled Fusako's head with words in English, she would understand and speak English back, like filling a bucket with water then pouring it back out again. Mildred also decided on the second day that they would call her Suzy, not Fusako.

At the end of the fifth day, when they turned off the Nacogdoches highway Mildred began to point to everything they passed, teaching Suzy everything about her new home. Wesley drove them down the narrow sand road that led from the Nacogdoches highway to the place where they worked the fields on the halves for old man Hart. "Suzy, look here, that's the Briley Town Missionary Baptist Church. Can you say church? And right up here is the old Hart cemetery. And in a little bit we'll be going by the Deloney place. They're our closest neighbors."

They turned from the road onto the long narrow lane that ran along the barbed wire fence to the clump of trees in front of their house. "Look, Suzy, this is where you are gonna live with me, my husband Carlos, and my boy Carlos."

Mildred noticed as they came to a stop in front of the house that the pick-up truck was gone. She was sure, since it was Sunday and the only day they didn't work, their son must have gone fishing down at the river to get away from his daddy for a few hours.

"Wesley, honk the horn a couple of times. Carlos might be out at the barn." Mildred jumped out and ran around to Suzy's side of the car and opened the door. "Git out, Suzy, git out. We're home. This is home. Home." Mildred pulled Suzy from the car and led her to the bottom of the steps. "Carlos! We're home. Come out and meet Suzy."

She turned to look at the barn then heard footsteps in the hallway that ran through the center of the house. Carlos appeared behind the screen of the front door.

"We're home!"

Carlos stood with his hand on the door handle.

"Well, come on out. I want to introduce you to Suzy."

Mildred put her arm around Suzy's shoulders and guided her to the bottom porch step. Carlos stepped from behind the screen and onto the porch. He let the screen door slam behind him then leaned back against it.

"Mildred, don't bring her any closer. I don't want that dirty Jap bitch in my house."

Mildred pulled Suzy to her side. "Carlos, this is Brother's wife, widow. She's got to live with us. We said we'd take care of her. You said she could. That we would. We signed them affidavits with the government saying we would."

"I don't give a damn what I signed or who I signed it for. This is my house. I've been thinking while you was gone and hearing what people in town are saying. How are we supposed to go to town and see people, or go to church, and have people know we have a damned Jap living under our roof? What about the mommas and daddies of them boys that died in the war over there? What are you gonna say to them? And old man Adams in town even says most of them Japs have TB. You want us or our boy to catch something like that from her?"

Suzy looked up at Mildred's face. Mildred turned to Audrey standing by the car. "Audrey, come here. Take Suzy over to the barn to look at the mules in the lot. I bet she's never seen a mule before."

Mildred walked up the steps to Carlos's side. "Carlos, we can't do this. We done agreed."

"I don't care what we agreed. I won't have no Jap in the same house with me. You can make a choice right now. You can side with her or you can side with your own family."

"But Carlos, she *is* family." Mildred lifted the hem of her skirt and wiped tears from her face. "She's our sister-in-law. She's my dead brother's wife, the last thing I have of him."

"You might as well just git on out of here, cause I'm not changing my mind. See if your daddy or one of your brothers or sisters will take her in."

Carlos walked back inside the house and slammed both doors behind him. Mildred heard the rattle as he turned the skeleton key to lock the heavy wooden door.

September 1951

Mildred felt something shift in her heart when Carlos turned the skeleton key in the lock in the front door of their house, barring her and her sister-in-law from entering.

What she thought was an endless well of love for him finally ran dry. As if the earth had shifted deep down and a had fissure formed, draining away the love she thought she had for him. And then, like in the Bible story, scales fell from her eyes and she saw him for what he was.

She was no longer blind to the futility of her love for him. She had wasted her life on a worthless cause. After twenty years of marriage, she knew she would not spend another night in the same house with him. No amount of love would make him different. The day she had waited for, when all the love she had provided him would turn his heart, would never come. As easily as she had fallen in love with the man she thought needed her so badly, her love ended.

At once she saw revealed before her all the misery and pain he, his father, and now her own son, had caused in the world. And she had, in her own way, allowed it to continue. She had had her doubts before, but this was the first time that she saw it all clearly. She was ready to turn her back on these men and their world and their ways and begin again.

If there was a God and He was sending all this to her because of what she did to that baby, when she knew she had done the right thing, then she didn't want to believe in Him.

She was going to test Him now. She would see if He would bless her doing something that she knew more than anything in the world was righteous. If He didn't bless this she could no longer believe in anything.

Mildred recalled the steps she took all those years before when departing from Carlos near her father's house, how she thought her love could provide what he needed. Now, she turned her back to Carlos and walked the same number of steps, this time to her brother's car, to be taken away from this man forever.

In Suzy's frightened eyes, she recognized the same expression she had seen on the face of that young woman on a sidewalk in Houston, and she recognized it as the same expression she had seen on her own face many times before, as she stood in front of a mirror washing her face after crying. She would bring these three women together, and they would never again shape their face out of grief and fear and anger and shame from the men in their lives.

And now there was the baby boy, born in shame and rejected by its daddy, her son. She wanted to shield that boy from the men in the family and make sure that he did not become a man like his father, or his father's father, or his father's father's father.

All the nervous energy and drive that had allowed her to be her husband's slave for all those years, she would direct to that boy and the women she would gather around her.

Since the last thing she would do was move back in with her own father, Mildred turned to the only man she knew who might be able to help her: Mister Foshay. Mister Foshay had a friend, a Mister Beal, who owned a café near the courthouse in Nacogdoches. He was a big fat man, even fatter than Mister Foshay, who always played Santa for the orphan's home at Christmas. He had once joked with Mildred when she and Carlos had dinner in the café that if she ever needed a job he would hire her in a New York minute.

After one night at her sister's house, Mildred found a ride into Nacogdoches. Within an hour, Mister Beal had given her a job at the café and even offered a place for her and Suzy to live.

Mister Beal's mother in law had recently died, and her little house at the back of the house he shared with his wife was empty. The little house sat in the back corner of the yard of one of the big brick houses on Raguet Street, within walking distance of the café. His mother in law lived there for the last twenty years of her life, teaching piano to almost every child in the neighborhood.

The house was enough and her job was enough. For the first time, Mildred was responsible for her own life. Mildred taught Suzy English the way she taught a baby to speak. She pointed at things and gave their names. She and Suzy worked on Suzy's English when Mildred was home between shifts. Within a month, Mildred had convinced Mister Beal to hire Suzy to work at the café. He wasn't sure at first how his customers would respond to a Japanese waitress, but Suzy's moon-round face and sweet nature soon won them over. And the story of her lost husband, a war hero and Mildred's brother, convinced them of her goodness, despite her native country.

The customers of the café soon heard the story of how Carlos had turned the women away from his house. The courthouse employees always tipped Fusako and Mildred a bit more generously than they normally would, knowing that the women were on their own and only had one another. Wearing matching white uniforms and white nurse shoes, the women soon became the center of the café's life.

As soon as she and Suzy were settled into their little house, Mildred approached Mister Beal with her plan. She wanted to bring Lois and the baby up from Houston to live in the little house. She assured him there was space enough for them all. She and Suzy would ask Lois to join them and they would all raise the baby together.

October 1951

Lois thought of the night ahead as she walked out of the front door of the five and dime store.

No baby. Not tonight. Rest at last, the first in seven months.

Lois was tired. Tired of taking care of the baby. Tired of working two jobs. Tired of being alone. Except for a single dollar, the money was long gone. Lois had decided that Mildred hadn't found a solution to her problem and wouldn't be coming for her. She was on her own and had to make her way, with the baby, the best she could.

It was six o'clock. She walked the two blocks from McCrory's to the rented room she shared with her son. But the baby would not be there tonight. That thought was the only relief in sight.

Nell, her neighbor across the hall, had insisted on keeping the baby so Lois could get a good night's sleep. The night before, Nell had found Lois asleep on the stairs halfway between the third and fourth floors.

Lois had to be at work at the dry cleaners at six the next morning and would not see her son for almost forty-eight hours.

Lois envied her neighbor. Nell's husband was fighting in Korea. She received a check from him each month that meant Nell didn't have to work two jobs. Nell never had to worry about the looks she received coming and going from the hotel. Lois felt that everyone could tell just by looking at her that she wasn't married and had a bastard child at home. She walked quickly and avoided making eye contact with people on the sidewalks of the city. If people mistakenly thought Lois had a husband too and that he was in Korea or dead, she wasn't going to set them straight.

Since the baby came, Lois lived her life in this room, four steps wide with two small windows over the street. Stained yellow curtains hid broken blinds. A dirty brown rug, a small table and two chairs, a chest of drawers, a narrow bed with an iron frame. A porcelain sink attached to the wall. A dresser with a hotplate. A tin breadbox for keeping roaches away from the food and a small refrigerator that hummed and rattled next to the sink. And now the baby's bed. The bathroom Lois shared with the other residents of the floor was at the far end of the hallway.

Tonight, without the baby, she had the room to herself. She reveled in the silence. No movement outside her own. No need except her own. Lois cleaned the room, changed into a robe and slippers, walked down the hall and took a long bath. She returned to the room, heated a can of soup and ate it with iced tea and two slices of white bread. She washed her dishes, put them away, then sat on the bed. She sighed and took a breath deeper than any she had in at least a year.

A knock at the door.

Lois opened the peephole. All she could see was the top of a man's shirt, the tan skin in the V just below his Adam's apple. She couldn't see his face. He was too close to the door. "Who is it?"

"It's me. Carlos. You know who it is."

She opened the door.

He stood with his legs wide apart, his hands hanging at his sides. She was certain he was wearing the same shirt and dungarees as the night they met. He looked over her head into the room, so she opened the door wider. "Momma told me to come and get you," he said.

"What? Well, come on in."

She stepped back into the room. He walked in and stood with his back against the wall just inside the door.

"You know, until just now I've never been upstairs higher than the second story. Even in the courthouse in Nacogdoches."

"How did you find us?"

"Momma told me how to get here. I think she's been talking to Mister Otto and your grandmomma. They must've known how to find you and told her. My momma and daddy have done separated. Momma is living down in Nacogdoches with her Jap sister-in-law. She just told me to come and get you, bring you and the baby back up to her. She didn't say anything else and I didn't ask, so don't ask me nothing else because I won't know the answer."

"Can I get you something to drink? All I have is some tea or milk. Or water."

"No, I'm fine. You want me to wait in the pickup?"

"You mean you want me to get us ready and leave now?"

"Yeah. If I'm gonna do this, you need to get yawl ready and let's go."

"What do you mean, come to get us?"

"I just come to get yawl and bring you to where my Momma is living in Nacogdoches."

"But where is home supposed to be?"

"Don't worry about that. Momma just told me to come and get yawl and bring you back to her. She didn't give me no choice."

Lois walked to the center of the room and turned back toward him. "I can't just leave like this. I have to give my quit notice at both my jobs, get my last pay, talk to Missus King, and settle up with her on the money I owe for keeping the baby. It's too late tonight. And I need to tell my landlord. I have to get the baby from Nell."

"Well, Daddy is expecting me back to work in the morning. If we're going to go we have to do it now."

"Hold on. I have to think about this a minute." Lois took a deep breath. "Don't you even want to see the baby? You haven't even asked about him. Did you even know he was a boy? I sent you a letter but you never answered."

"I'll see it when we're heading home. I don't like this place. I'm gonna go buy some gas at the filling station I saw down the road a piece. Be ready when I get back."

"Be ready? I haven't heard a thing from you and now you show up and want us to go with you?"

"This is the one chance you get. I won't be back, I promise you that. I'll be waiting out front after I get the gas. And I won't wait long. If you are coming, you better have the baby and your stuff and be ready by the time I get back."

They drove to Nacogdoches in silence. Carlos left Lois standing at the curb, the boy on her hip and two suitcases at her feet. She watched him drive away, then turned and looked up the driveway, beyond the big brick house near the street, to the little clapboard cottage that stood beside the carport. Carlos had pointed at the little house and said, there it is, Momma and the Jap will be waiting for you. He had never been any closer to the little house than the street.

Balancing the boy on her hip, Lois lifted the suitcases, walked up the driveway and to the house at the back of the yard. She knocked on the door and waited.

1956

Carlos lay on his back and looked up at the taut cloud of pale green fabric suspended above him. He could touch it if his arms were just a little longer. His grandmother sat to his left, his mother to his right, her left hand tucked under the frame, and his great-aunt at the end of the frame near his feet. With her left hand tucked under the frame, his mother caught the needle as it pierced the fabric from above. Although he couldn't see it, he knew her other hand hovered on the top side of the fabric, her elbow resting on the wooden frame. Her fingers sent the needle and thread down. To the boy, it was magic; as if her left hand, beneath the frame, was magnetic and attracted the needle from above. He marveled at how his mother spaced the stitches, made them precisely the same size. She seemed to follow an invisible pattern only known to her, creating geometry where before there had been only an expanse of colored fabric.

Carlos loved these afternoons with his mother, aunt, and grandmother, when after their shifts at the café or canning whatever was in season, they stole minutes in the quiet afternoon to quilt and talk. They moved the furniture from the center of the room and his mother stood on a chair to hang the quilt frame from the four hooks in the ceiling of the living room.

They were almost finished with this quilt. It was not a particu-
larly large one, but there had been so little time to work on it. They
began early in the New Year with the scraps from their fall sewing,
printed cottonseed sacks, and any scraps other women gave them.
They sat opposite each other, using small patterns made from brown
grocery bags to cut out the shapes of the scraps. By early February
they sewed the scraps into patterned blocks. At Easter, they worked
together on sewing the blocks together into the quilt top. Then they
hung the frame from the ceiling to do their quilting work. They
combed the cotton themselves and placed it between the patchwork
top and the solid colored bottom.

Carlos beat his bare heels against the rug, his fingers laced behind his head.

"You alright under there, Honey?"

"Yeah, Granny."

"You wanna do some quiltin, Sweet Thing?" He didn't respond.
"Sugar? Come out from under there and stand here next to Granny
so I can help you."

"No, Mam, I wanna do it from down here."

The women continued with their work. "Now Sugar, you know
I can't show you where to put the needle to do the next stitch from
down there."

"Then I don't wanna do it."

"Okay then, Sweet Man, suit yourself."

They continued to quilt, silent for the moment, concentrating on
their work.

Carlos didn't like the silence. And he knew that the women hated silence too. They usually filled the air with words, to keep their
minds occupied in the same way the quilting kept their hands busy.
They retold stories just to keep the silence at bay.

"Lois, reach over behind you and get me one of those big scraps.
I'll set him up sewing on his own."

His mother's hand disappeared from under the frame and he
heard the swoosh of fabric on fabric as she tossed the scrap across
the frame to Mildred. Mildred's hand disappeared from under the

frame, then reappeared in her lap, offering a small square of fabric.

"Now, take this, Baby. You can do your own sewing. I gave you a big old needle to make it easier for you. I tied a knot in the end of your thread and done made a couple of stitches. Your momma and Aunt Suzy and me will be done in just a little bit. You've been such a goodun today. Now you make Granny a play pretty or something. If you get sleepy you could rest your eyes too. You want Granny to get you a little quilt to cover with?"

"No, Mam, thank you."

His grandmother laughed.

"Would you listen to those fine manners that boy has. Lois, I think we got a real gentleman on our hands."

"And in a minute, if we are good, he's gonna get up and tell us one of his made-up stories. Maybe one of those about the prince living in the castle with his momma, granny, and aunt. Might you, Baby? That boy can make up stories better than anybody. Can't you, Baby?"

He sat up, took the cloth from his grandmother and began his work. He made a few stitches, then lay back again. With his arms outstretched from his sides and his feet crossed at the ankles, he dipped his chin toward his right shoulder, trying to remember the exact pose of Jesus on the cross in the Bible on his grandmother's dresser. He rested one hand on his mother's ankle, his other hand on his grandmother's foot, and pointed his toes and rested them on his Aunt Suzy's slipper. They didn't move or say a word, but he knew they were sharing smiles above the field of fabric over his head.

1958

Suzy walked into the house and found Mildred sitting in front of a box fan with an enamel dishpan on her lap, her hands busy shelling peas. A bushel basket sat on each side of her rocking chair, one half full of purple-hulled peas and the other half-filled with the wet husks of pods already shelled. Suzy sat down in a chair next to the basket of unshelled peas.

"Mildred, I want to talk to you about something. Something important."

Mildred met Suzy's eyes. "Well, I sure hope it ain't nothing bad. It ain't money trouble, is it? Or the boy?"

"No, it's something good important."

"If it's something good then don't tarry in tellin me."

"It's about a man."

"What do you mean about a man?"

"It's a secret about a man, a secret man that I need to tell you about."

Mildred dropped a half-shelled pod into the dish pan and looked at Suzy. "Go on. I'm listening."

"I've been scared to tell you about him because I know what you think of most of the men from around here."

"With good reason, you know."

"I waited to tell you until it got serious."

"You aren't in any kind of trouble, are you?"

"No, it's not anything like that. You know me better than that."

"Well, what is it then?"

"It's just that it's getting serious and I wanted you to meet him and know him." Suzy turned toward the screen door that led out unto the carport. "He's out there waiting. He wants to meet and talk to you. But I think you already know him, since you know just about everybody in the county."

"Who is he?"

"Jimmy Daughtry. He says he's known your people since he was little and even knows your son. His daddy is James Daughtry. They live out toward Martinsville somewhere."

"Yeah, I know him, his daddy too. But what's he got to say to me other than howdy?"

"I don't know, Mildred. He just wants to talk to you."

"He can come down to the café to talk to me anytime he wants. I sure don't need to meet him here and talk about something you don't even know about."

"Mildred, I'm sure you will like him. He was in the war in Europe, like Weldon. He's seen some of the world and ain't just any boy from Nacogdoches county, like you've warned me about. Please talk to him. He's waiting."

"Well you can send him in, but I've only got a minute. You can see I'm busy shelling and putting up all these peas for Missus Beal."

Suzy walked out the door onto the carport and returned with a young man at her side. He was tall and thin, with a narrow face and blue eyes. He wore a short-sleeved plaid shirt, blue jeans, a brown leather belt with a large silver buckle, and cowboy boots. He held a straw hat in his left hand. Suzy stood beside him, her shoulder level with the young man's navel, the top of her head at his chest. Mildred stared at his hand resting on Suzy's shoulder. "Mildred, this is Jimmy Daughtry. Jimmy, this is Miss Mildred Dews."

"Miss Mildred, it's mighty nice to see you again. You might remember me from when I was a boy. Me and my daddy used to come to see Mister Carlos on the Langston place."

Jimmy lifted his hand from Suzy's shoulder, stepped forward, and offered it to Mildred. She lifted her hands, palms up, wet with pea juice, and shook her head. He lowered his hand to his side.

"Suzy, would you mind stepping outside and let me talk to Miss Mildred?"

Suzy looked at Jimmy then Mildred.

"Go on, Suzy, let me and Jimmy have a little talk."

"Okay. I'll wait out on the porch swing under the carport. Jimmy, come get me when you are done." Suzy walked out the screen door, letting it slam behind her.

Jimmy watched Suzy disappear around the side of Mister Beal's car, then turned back to face Mildred. He held his hat in both hands, covering his large belt buckle.

"I sure do appreciate you meeting me and letting me talk with you a bit. Suzy told me she's done told you that we've been courtin. Well, I've got something to ask you."

He shifted his weight between his feet. Mildred looked down at the pan in her lap, lifted a purple pod, shelled it, and picked up another. Jimmy bowed his head to watch her hands as he spoke.

"Miss Mildred, I know Suzy don't have no people left, and I sure would appreciate it if you would say it was okay for me to marry her. I think she is the prettiest thing I've ever seen. Known it since the first time I saw her in the café. I love her and want to marry her. I sure do think she would make a mighty fine wife."

Mildred looked up and met the young man's eyes.

"Jimmy, would you please go get Suzy and send her back in to see me."

"Miss Mildred? I don't understand. You haven't answered my question. We just started talking, and I sure would like to get an answer from you before I ask Suzy to marry me."

"And you stay out there until I'm done talking with her."

He turned and walked out the door.

Mildred shelled peas and waited. She heard the mumbles of a

conversation between Suzy and Jimmy as they stood just out of sight at the front of the carport.

Suzy returned. "How well do you know this Daughtry boy?"

"We been going out together for a few months now. When we could find time when we weren't both working and when I had a good excuse to be out of the house, without you knowing what I was doing."

"Do you know what he just asked me?"

"I didn't until he just told me now outside."

"Do you love this Daughtry boy? Do you love him the way you did Brother?"

"I do. It ain't exactly like with Weldon but it's good. He says he loves me. That's what I need."

"He don't love you. He called you a girl and he says he loved you the first time he saw you. This means he loves some idea in the world that you remind him of. There's something about you that reminds him of something he's already lost, or is missing. He don't really know you."

"But Mildred, even if that's true, we love each other. I feel it."

"You can't go off with the first man who asks you to marry him. And what about the boy? When we agreed to take in Lois and the baby, we promised each other we would see this through together. See him grown."

"Yes, Mildred, but that didn't mean forever. And the boy is already seven years old. You and Lois are doing fine and can take care of him. You'll even have more space in the house without me here. And it's not like I'm going far away. I'll still be in the county and I might even be able to keep working at the café, if Jimmy says it's okay, and help you with the boy when you need it. I appreciate what you have done for me, but—"

"You go out there and tell that boy that he ain't to talk to you ever again. If you won't, I will. And if you like him as much as you say, you probably don't want me to do it for you. Tell him he ain't welcomed at the café anymore, either. You are my responsibility and I won't let you make a mistake like this."

Suzy sat down in the chair next to Mildred and began to cry. "But Mildred, I'm afraid that no man will have me. Many think I'm pretty, but most of them or their families wouldn't let them marry me. Just like Carlos, they say Japanese people are sick with TB or something else and they think I had something to do with all them boys killed in the war. I might not get another offer."

"That ain't no reason to marry a man, just because you're afraid the right kind of man won't come along."

"Mildred, you are the only sister I'll ever have. I'm not sure I'd be alive today without you. You saved me and brought me to this country. But I want love. I want to have what me and Weldon had."

"Then wait till you find that."

"Mildred. You are like my sister but you aren't my mother. You can't make me stay."

"If you go with that boy, I can tell you what your life will be like in three years. I know these people, especially the men. And you don't. I've known them my whole life. You don't know these boys like I do. I know what they want. They want to sleep with you at night, have babies with you, yes, but mostly they want someone to take care of them. They want a house nigger, somebody to take care of everything in their lives so they don't have to. They want a mother, a whore, and a slave all in one. And what do you think you will get in exchange for being that for them? Now you go out there and send that boy away from here. If you don't, I sure will."

Mildred moved the dish pan from her lap and placed it on top of the bushel of peas at her side. She bent forward as if to stand.

Suzy jumped from the chair and ran out the screen door. Mildred heard the mumble of another conversation. It faded as Suzy and Jimmy walked from the carport down the driveway toward the street. She heard the squeal of tires as Jimmy drove away.

Suzy ran back through the screen door, passed Mildred and slammed the door of the bedroom they shared.

1960

Carlos rested on the space behind the back seat of the high-finned Cadillac, under the car's back glass, watching the tops of the piney woods of East Texas pass above him, the breaks between the branches allowing glimpses of a bright blue sky. His grandmother had borrowed the car from Mister Beal at the café. As the car sped northeast from Nacogdoches County toward the town of Terrell, Suzy, Mildred, and Lois rode in silence and listened to the radio. Sad country songs, reports on cattle prices, and the rare local news. The hair of the boy's crew cut vibrated from the speaker directly under his head. The music and talk of the radio interrupted only by Mildred's "Pick up your feet, Sugar" every time they crossed a bridge, or "Look at that cow out there, yawl" whenever she wanted to distract the other women long enough to insert or remove her false teeth without an audience.

They stopped at a familiar roadside barbeque stand halfway to Terrell, where they ate pork sandwiches dripping with hot sauce and the sweetest onions and sourest pickles they had ever tasted. They washed down the sandwiches with Coca-Cola then continued the drive. Carlos returned to his spot behind the back seat of the car and slept until they arrived at the cemetery.

She was buried just outside the barbed wire fence of the Texas State Mental Hospital, on the outskirts of Terrell. When Mildred pulled over to the side of the highway Carlos jumped from the car to open the gate of the chain link fence that separated the cemetery from the surrounding hay fields. Mildred drove the car through the gate, parked under a large cedar tree, and took a pot of plastic flowers from the trunk of the car. Lois carried a paper grocery bag of cleaning supplies that had sat between her feet in the floorboard of the car. Suzy carried an old quilt she took from the back seat of the car.

Her stone was easy to find because most of the graves were without markers. Saving extra tip money from the café and the little they made shelling peas and quilting, Mildred, Lois, and Suzy had bought the headstone for her the year after the boy was born.

As Suzy spread the quilt on the grass next to the grave, Lois removed a mayonnaise jar of soapy water and a rag from the grocery bag and scrubbed the tombstone. Mildred replaced the pot of faded flowers from their visit the previous year with a new pot of bright plastic. She placed it directly below the name carved into the stone: *Sarah Dews 1880-1927.*

The first time the women visited her grave, when the boy was just a baby, they had learned from a decent man in the hospital office the exact spot where she was buried. No one knew the year she was born, not even her daughter, so they had picked a nice round number for the stone, figuring she was probably around seventeen years old when Carlos and his twin were born in 1897.

Carlos was the only member of her family, with her blood flowing through his veins, to have ever visited her grave.

After cleaning the tombstone and pulling the weeds that had grown for a year on the grave, they sat for a long time in the shade of a sweet gum tree, thinking about Sarah and wondering what she had thought for the nineteen years when she was living and dying in the asylum up the hill from where they sat.

Just before they stood to pack up the things to begin their trip back to Nacogdoches, Mildred told, for the first time, a story she heard years before, whispered to her by her husband's sister, of what had happened the last time they saw their mother.

1908

Cordelia woke with her mother's hand on her shoulder and her mother's lips pressed to her right ear.

"Get up, honey, it's time."

Her mother turned back the sheet into a perfect triangle and Cordelia stepped down out of the bed. Her mother placed a finger over her lips, pointed to Carlos, still asleep in the bed next to where Cordelia had been sleeping, and shook her head. Cordelia tiptoed after their mother out the door of the small room.

In the dogtrot hallway, Cordelia sat on a chair as her mother tied her shoes. The woman and her daughter moved silently as they walked down the hallway to the porch that ran across the back of the house. They knew on which planks of the broad wood floor they could step without making any sounds and which would creak and give them away. They didn't need to speak because they had planned it all. And Sarah had tried this very thing many times before. But he always caught her and brought her back. This time would be different.

While Frank was plowing the field down by the creek the previous day, Sarah took Cordelia and walked down to the Williams's house.

Sarah barely knew Missus Williams because Frank didn't allow her to leave the house or talk to other women. As they walked to the Williams place Sarah looked over her shoulder toward the field where Frank was working.

The woman and her daughter walked up to the back door of the big white house. Sarah knocked then stood at the bottom of the steps. They could hear footsteps inside the house. A black face appeared behind the screen door.

"Yes, Mam, can I help you?"

"Yes, I'm Missus Dews, we live here on the place, we work the fields over on the Tonkawa Hill road. Could I please speak to Missus Williams?"

"Yes, Mam, I'll go get her. You just wait right here."

When Missus Williams came to the door, Sarah sent Cordelia to stand against the well curb at the corner of the yard. As the two women talked, Cordelia saw her mother lift the sleeves of her dress and pull up her skirt far enough for Missus Williams to see the bruises Frank had left the last time he beat her. Missus Williams put her hands up to her mouth and shook her head. Sarah then disappeared inside the house with Missus Williams.

Cordelia knew that things were changing. Her father's beatings of their mother were getting worse. She was afraid he might kill her. And Cordelia was afraid that Carlos was old enough now to try to stop him. Their father had begun to send Carlos away to do chores when he chose to beat their mother. He was always worse with their mother when Carlos wasn't around. Cordelia was certain that each time he beat her it got worse, more savage.

Cordelia knew their mother wasn't crazy as their father claimed. She couldn't do anything right in his eyes. And he beat her like a dog. Cordelia saw him once beat her so hard that blood ran out of her ears. He'd come in from the fields and she could just say one little thing wrong and he would fly all over her. Cordelia understood that their mother acted strange because she never knew which direction he was going to come from, what he was going to say she had done wrong, and what he was going to hit her with next.

On the way back home from the Williams place Sarah told Cordelia what she and Missus Williams had planned. That night, Sarah, Cordelia, and Carlos were to sneak out of the house and make their way down to the Williams place. Missus Williams told Sarah for them to hide in the tack barn next to the mule lot. Missus Williams would have her bachelor brother, a Mister John Lawson, give them a ride in his wagon up north of town where they could catch the train to Texarkana then up toward Oklahoma where Sarah's people lived. Missus Williams gave Sarah some money to help them make the trip.

That night, after dinner, Sarah had Cordelia gather some things together to take with them. She told Cordelia to make it look like she was getting things together to do the washing the next day. Frank never paid any attention to such things, so Sarah was sure he wouldn't figure out what was going on.

Cordelia didn't know what time it was as she followed her mother down the dogtrot. Her father kept their only timepiece on a chain in his pocket. But she knew it was very late. Her mother stepped off the back porch and walked out to the feed shed. Cordelia stood on the porch and watched as Sarah walked across the back yard. Sarah returned with two tow sacks for them to use for their clothes and things. A glint of moonlight off the ax head seemed to catch Sarah's attention, and she walked out of her way to the chop block. She pulled the ax out of the stump and brought it back to the house with her.

Cordelia stood in the dogtrot stuffing their few clothes into the tow sacks, and Sarah sat down in one of the chairs outside the door to the room where she and Frank slept. Sarah held the ax between her knees with its head resting on the floor between her feet.

Cordelia walked behind the chair and whispered, "Momma, I'm done with the clothes."

"You just wait right here, honey. Momma needs to get her clothes out of her room. We'll wait to wake up Carlos until we are ready to go. I don't want him having too much time to think about this. He might just tell your Daddy, or not want to go. I'll be back in a second and then we will go. You just wait right here now."

Sarah tiptoed to the door into the room where her husband slept and opened it carefully. She stepped inside and closed the door slowly behind her.

Cordelia walked to the back porch and to the window into her parents' room. Sarah walked over to the side of the bed where Frank slept. She grabbed the ax about halfway up the handle and lifted it above her head.

One of the floor boards underneath her squeaked and Frank opened his eyes.

He jumped to the side just as Sarah brought down the ax with all her strength. The ax head hit the edge of the pillow. Sarah held on to the ax and pulled it back to her. Frank jumped out of the bed on the side opposite her. With the ax held to her chest, the head just beneath her chin, she backed up into the corner of the room.

"Frank Dews, don't you touch me again or I'll kill you."

"Woman, you can just try. Now give me that goddamned ax."

They stood looking at each other. He took a slow step forward. Sarah turned quickly and ran toward the door.

Cordelia ran to the spot where the back porch met the dogtrot and looked through the center of the house. Her mother ran up the hallway, bumping into one of the chairs at the table where they ate. Her mother made it to the end of the hallway, to the door to the room where Cordelia and her brother slept. Cordelia saw her mother try to open the door when her father grabbed her by the arm and pulled her to him.

"My babies!"

It was all her mother said. Frank put his arms around her and she dropped the ax. They struggled. Sarah stomped on his foot and broke free. She ran down the front steps of the house and into the fields.

Cordelia watched down the length of the hallway as their father sat on the front steps putting on his boots and buckling the straps of his overalls. Carlos walked out of their room and into the dogtrot, tripping over the ax.

Cordelia's final image of her mother was the back edge of her white cotton gown brushing against the back of her knee as she tripped down the wooden front steps of the house and into the field. Her father rushed down the steps after her.

Cordelia walked to her brother's side and tugged on his night shirt. "Carlos, where's Momma?"

1962

Suzy and Mildred sat on the porch swing under the carport, drinking iced tea from sweating Mason jars. Suzy's feet didn't reach the concrete floor of the carport, so Mildred kept them in motion with the tips of her toes.

"It won't be long before I need to go in and start fixin our dinner. I thought I'd fry up some of that deer brisket and a mess of those pink-eyed purple-hulled peas. That and some cornbread and butter oughta do us fine tonight. Lois and the boy are gonna have their dinner at the café."

Suzy looked at her watch and turned to face Mildred. "Well, we might have a guest for dinner tonight, Mildred."

"A guest? What are you talking about, girl?"

"You remember Jimmy Daughtry? That boy that wanted to marry me a few years back? The one you made me run off?"

"Yes, Suzy. You know I remember that boy. And he better not be our guest tonight."

"No, he's not the guest, but I wanted you to remember that time with the Daughtry boy. You were right about him, and I wanted to tell you so. It took me a long time to realize that. I think I even hated you for a long time for that. But it turned out you was right. He ended up marrying that Welch girl that worked in the Mize clothes factory. She couldn't have any babies and he started beating her. Bad. And when we heard about it at the café you didn't say a word. You could have said I told you so, but you didn't."

Mildred pushed off with her toes to start the swing moving again. "I knew all along that Daughtry boy was bad. I knew his daddy and I knew how he would be. I didn't need to say I told you so because I knew you knew. I knew you would come around to see him the way I knew he was."

Suzy hopped off the swing and stood in front of Mildred. "But this time it's different, Mildred. I've found somebody else and I know he will be good to me. And if I'm wrong and he ain't I can only blame myself. I'm willing to accept that blame."

"Now Suzy, I know the crop you've got to choose from around here, and I see the men you talk to at the café."

"Well this one is different. Mildred, you have to let me do this. This man reminds me so much of your brother, and I feel just the same way about him that I did for Weldon. He's stopping by in a few minutes and I want you to meet him. Not to say yes or no to my choice, but to just meet him. I want you to know him because I'm sure you will like him. He is just about the sweetest man I've ever met. He has a job up in Dallas and wants us to get married and move up there together. His name is Allen Summers. You have to meet him."

Mildred stopped the swing with her toes. "I guess you ain't gonna give me a chance to say anything about it, Suzy." Suzy climbed back onto the swing next to Mildred.

"I want to know what you think, Mildred, but I won't let you say that I can't be with this man. I've waited and watched and hoped, for four long years. After that first time, I hated you because I was sure you were wrong. But I've learned something other than that you were right, in those years too. You've made me strong, Mildred. I wasn't ready before, and I know that now. You made me strong enough to know I don't need a man to live, but you also taught me to be strong enough to know when I want a man on my own, strong enough to tell even you that this is my choice. You know when I knew he was

right? I knew when I thought I'd sure like for him to have known
Weldon and for Weldon to have known him. They would have surely
been friends. That's when I knew."

Both women looked up at the sound of a car stopping in the
street in front of the house. "I bet that's him now. I'll be back with
him in a minute." Suzy jumped off the swing, ran out of the carport
and down the driveway toward the street.

Mildred started the swing with her toes. And waited.

Suzy returned with a young man at her side. They held hands as
they walked under the carport and stood in front of Mildred. The
young man wore khaki pants and a blue shirt, a brown leather belt
and matching shoes. He was thin, with crew cut dark hair and brown
eyes. He released his right hand from Suzy's and extended it to Mildred, and she took it.

"Miss Mildred, I'm Allen Summers. It is a pleasure to meet you.
I'm thankful for you agreeing to meet me like this."

"It's nice to meet you, Allen. Why don't you pull up that chair
and have a seat? Suzy, you wanna go in and make us a pot of coffee.
I'd like to speak with Mister Summers a minute."

The two women exchanged a long glance. Suzy went through
the screen door into the house. Mildred leaned forward, resting her
elbows on her knees. Allen sat in a lawn chair directly in front of her.

"Mister Summers, that girl means the world to me and I want
you to know it. She's like both a sister and a daughter to me."

"Yes, Mam, I know. She says that herself."

"And you know she was married to my brother who was killed in
the war?" The young man nodded. "I believe Suzy when she says
you will be good to her. But just in case you aren't, I want to tell you
that if I ever hear that you have mistreated her in any way, even if
she denies it, I will come and get her. Me and Suzy are like sisters
now, and she will always be a part of my life. Don't think that you
will ever be able to come between us. If you mistreat her in any way
you will have to answer to me. I may be little and look weak, but I
can handle a gun and you can't hide forever. You ever hurt her, you
are a dead man."

Allen lowered his head and looked at his feet. He began to cry.

"Miss Mildred, I've heard every word you've ever said. My daddy has told me about you for years. He always calls you Miss Mildred, and he's told me about you and how you took in Suzy when Mister Dews wouldn't take her in after your brother died. My momma and daddy both have lots of respect for you and told me, even before I came up here to see you today, that you were a good woman. That's the very words my daddy said. He said that Miss Mildred is a good woman. I'm so sorry that Suzy and I have been hiding that we were going out. I wanted to meet you months ago, but Suzy told me we should wait."

Allen looked up at Mildred.

"I have a university degree I got from the GI Bill of Rights, and I'm making something of myself. I've got a good offer of a job up in Dallas and I mean to take it. And it sure would mean a lot to me if you would say it was okay for me and Suzy to get married and move up there together. I promise that I will take care of her. I'll work every day of my life to make sure she has the best life possible. I know she's had a hard time in life. Losing her whole family in the war, then the trouble she had in Japan before you was able to bring her over here. I saw a lot of bad things in the war myself over in the Europe, and I want me and Suzy to have a good life so that we can just turn the page on all of that and never have to think about it. And Miss Mildred, I have one more question for you."

"What is it, Allen?"

"I haven't mentioned this, even to Suzy, but I was thinking that once we are married a while and have some time together, that if we are lucky enough to have a little boy, I sure would like to have your brother's name as part of our boy's name. Would you be okay with us doing that? I sure wish I had known your brother. It sounds like he was a fine man. And I know I can never be that good for Suzy, and you, but I'll sure try."

Mildred didn't answer. Allen looked up at her. With tears in her eyes, she nodded. She swallowed hard and turned toward the screen door. "Suzy, how is that coffee coming?"

Suzy came to the door. "It's about to boil."

"Leave it be and come on out here."

Mildred got up from the swing and stood next to Allen. "Suzy, you and Allen don't need me to tell you this is the right thing to do. It is and you already know it."

Suzy threw herself into Mildred's arms.

Mildred walked into the house to cook their dinner. Suzy and Allen sat on the porch swing. He pushed off with his brown leather shoes to start it swinging.

1962

"Mildred?"

She could tell from the tone of Lois's voice that something was wrong. Behind the counter of the café, a tray of open glass containers on the counter in front of her and a pitcher in her hand, Mildred was filling each container to its brim with sugar. She looked up to see Lois backing down the length of the counter toward her, her eyes on the man standing just inside the door. From the fear on Lois's face Mildred thought he might have a gun in his hand.

Lois backed up to the door into the kitchen and disappeared behind it.

Mildred almost didn't recognize her husband. It had been almost ten years since she and Suzy were driven away from the Hart place and she saw him from behind the screen door. The man standing inside the café door didn't look like the man she last saw slamming the door. She looked him up and down; he was in fact her husband.

When they lived together, Carlos would never have been seen in public in such a state. He had always insisted that Mildred keep his clothes clean. And the shoes he wore to town always had to be polished. Before going into town, he had always changed into his best overalls and boots and oiled and combed his hair.

The ramrod straight posture he had come to have while they were married was now gone. He stooped, his dark hair now streaked with gray. His face was pale with hollow cheeks. The stripped blue overalls, much too large for his once-solid frame, were dirty, with a hole in the right knee. His Brogan boots were coated in dust, and their toes were scuffed.

Mildred spoke before she had a chance to think. "Carlos? Don't just stand there blocking the door. Somebody might want to come in. Come on in and sit down someplace."

"Thank you, Mildred." Carlos sat down in the booth nearest the door, next to the cash register.

It was a Saturday afternoon, and the café was empty. Mildred put the pitcher of sugar on the counter next to the tray and, keeping the counter between them, walked near the booth where Carlos sat. "What do you want, Carlos? Why are you here?"

"I need to talk to you about some things."

"Is it our boy? Is something wrong? Has he gone and got himself killed, or in trouble?"

"No, Sugar. It's not about Carlos. You heard from him?"

"No, I thought he was probably still living with you, working the Hart place. Why? He ain't?"

"No, we had a falling out over a gal he wanted to bring to live with us and he done moved up toward Henderson. He's living with her and her people up there. He ain't ever come in the café to see you or nothing?"

"Carlos, he won't do that when he knows he might run into Lois and maybe even their boy."

"Mildred, I need to ask you something. A favor. But first, I have to tell you something."

Carlos put his elbows on the table and laced his fingers in front of his face. He looked at his hands.

"Mildred, I'm dying. I've got cancer of the urine bladder. It's done spread all over me, too. My insides are ate up with it." Mildred leaned onto the counter toward him. "The doctor don't know how much more time I got. Said it depends on how tough I am with it.

He's already done a couple of operations on me, but he's stopped trying that now. You can see I'm wasting away, and I'm pretty weak."

"You okay, Mildred?" Lois stood in the door to the kitchen.

"Yeah, Lois, I'm fine." Lois disappeared back behind the swinging kitchen door. "Carlos, what do you want me to say?"

"I don't want you to say anything. I told you I had something to tell you and something to ask you. I've told you, now I need to ask you something. The favor."

Mildred walked from behind the counter and stood by his booth. "Go ahead, Carlos."

He took a deep breath. "I know I was bad to you and our boy. I have a feeling this cancer I got is a punishment from God for me being such a son of a bitch. But things are different now, Mildred. It won't be the same as it was before." He looked up at her. "Sit down here with me, Mildred. I don't want to talk to you about this with you standing over me. Sit down here across from me."

Mildred sat down in the booth opposite him. He lowered his voice. "I'm not even a man anymore. One of the doctor's operations did that to me. You understand what I'm saying? I ain't interested in no women no more. Can't be interested. And I bet that's from that damned Babtist God too. I have a place of my own. Anybody already told you I bought part of the old Nall place? Even have a little house of my own on it. I've been raising a big truck patch every year and have a few cattle and a hay meadow and a good barn. It's been enough for me for the past few years."

"That's nice, Carlos. You always wanted a place of your own so you wouldn't have to be working for nobody else anymore."

"Well, I finally got that. It's a nice little place. I've nearly killed myself working it by myself. But it's a nice little place now." Carlos put his hands palms down on the table between them. "I wanted to ask if you'd be able to forgive me enough to come to stay with me down on the place. Just long enough to see me on out. To take care of me here at the end, so I could stay on the place and not have to go to no hospital or nothing. And in trade, I'd leave the place and the cattle to you when I'm gone. When I die, you'd have the place to yourself. So, if you wanted, you and the girl and her boy and your sister-in-law could all get away from here in town and all live down there on the place all together."

The door to the café opened and a man and a woman walked in. Mildred turned toward the kitchen. "Lois, can you come on out and wait on these fine folks?" She turned to the man and woman. "She'll be right out to help you."

Lois came out of the kitchen and directed the couple to a table at the opposite end of the café.

"So, what do you think, Mildred?"

Mildred took a deep breath and looked into Carlos's eyes. "Carlos, if you can't tell by just looking at me, I'm not the same Mildred I was before. Living on my own, joining with Suzy and Lois to raise that boy, has changed me. I know what is important and what ain't. I don't need another single soul in the world, and I sure don't need somebody needing me to make me happy. I nearly killed myself when we was together. You nearly killed me. And I hadn't done a thing to deserve it either. I was your momma and your wife and your whore. You didn't appreciate it and didn't give me nothing in exchange."

Mildred began to cry as she saw pain in Carlos's face. She swallowed and continued. "I never was able to stand up for myself before. But I can now." She took a deep breath and looked at the table top in front of her.

"You hurt me so bad, Carlos Dews. Nearly worked me and our boy to death, then just turned me and my sister-in-law out like stray dogs. And now you come back to me, when you're dying and need me again and ask me to take care of you?" Carlos covered his face with his hands. "Yeah, I could give Mister Beal my quit notice here and come back to take care of you. I could sure do it. But every cup of coffee I'd make for you would be full of hate, and we would both know it. Every time I held your arm to help you make it to the toilet, you'd wonder if I was gonna push you down the steps, or if my hate for you would cause that cancer to grow even faster. I could help you. I've got it in my power to do so. But I'm not. Every time you feel a pain from that cancer growing inside you I want you to think about all the pain you ever caused me and our boy. Think about all those mornings you made us get up before daylight and plow until after the sun went down that evening, telling Mister Hart you didn't need no other help. Think about all them women you were fucking when I was at home waiting on you and trying to have your babies."

Carlos looked toward the couple in the booth at the other end of the café.

"You think about the friends I could have had to make the hard times a little easier to take but no you wouldn't let me have any friends. It may seem mighty hard-hearted of me and God may send me to hell for it, but the answer is no. I'm proud of you for having your own place, and I'm so sorry you are sick. Nobody deserves that kind of pain and suffering. But the answer is no."

Carlos slid to the end of the booth and stood, using his hands on the edge of the table to push himself up. Mildred stood at the door of the café and watched Carlos disappear down the sidewalk in front of the courthouse, his shoulders stooped and his overalls moving loosely around his thin frame. Lois walked to Mildred's side and slipped her arm around her waist.

1963

On Carlos's twelfth birthday, his grandmother moved a trunk from the closet of the room that she shared with his mother into his bedroom. She sat it at the end of his bed and told him it was now his. He understood from the tone of his grandmother's voice that he was to revere what he found inside it.

That night, after his birthday dinner, the cake, the presents, and the singing of happy birthday, using the black leather handle at one end of the trunk, he pulled it to the center of his room and sat on the floor in front of it. The trunk was painted dark green and had tarnished brass corners. A blackened strip of metal ran along its edges. A name was stenciled in fading gold letters on its lid. *Lt. James Weldon Scogin, U.S. Army.* A yellowing address tag attached by thin wire hung from the leather strap at one end. He opened the rusty latch and lifted the lid.

Its contents filled only a third of the trunk.

A large envelope sat on top. In it he found a death certificate. *Florence Little Scogin. Cause of death: exsanguination/childbirth.* Next to her name was an asterisk and along the bottom of the page, following another asterisk, were five words. *And stillborn child, umbilical intact.*

Below this envelope he found small bundles of letters tied together by twine. These were the letters between his grandmother and her brother during World War II in Europe and in Japan and Korea. Some of his letters were handwritten on pale blue stationery; others were typed on tiny pieces of brown paper with the seal of the U.S. War Department and a seal with the word "V-mail" at the top. Hers were all written in pencil, mostly on white stationery, but a few were on paper with a flowery border or written inside and on the backs of birthday and Christmas cards.

Beneath the letters he found a newspaper folded to an interior page with a photograph of his mother, grandmother, and great-aunt, with broad smiles, standing beneath the sign of the Old Stone Fort Café, the place they had all worked for many years and where his mother and grandmother still worked every day.

Under the newspaper he found a heart-shaped candy box with words written in pen on its lid. *Things with Brother when he died.*

Each of the items inside was wrapped in cellophane faded to the color of iced tea. A watch with a green cloth band, black face and white numbers. A razor that opened like the gaping mouth of a baby bird when its handle was turned. Three rusty razor blades, a collection of coins, and some brightly colored paper money. The only words he could read on the money were "Bank of Korea." Another packet held thin bars covered in stripes of bright colored fabric with pins on their backs.

Beneath this candy box were four rectangular leather boxes that reminded the boy of the boxes that held watches in the window of the jewelry store on Main Street. Lined with white satin, these boxes each contained a single military medal, each hanging from a satin ribbon. One gold star, one silver star, and two gold hearts with the silhouette of the man he recognized as George Washington centered in the heart on a purple enamel background. He knew these medals already because his grandmother sometimes brought them from her room to her rocking chair in the living room. She would sit in her chair, drink coffee, and cry with the four boxes opened and resting on her thighs, two medals on each leg reaching from the bend of her housecoat at her lap to the precipice of her knees. She only did this when she knew Aunt Suzy had just begun a long shift at the café and wouldn't be home for hours.

Under the medals, in a brown legal envelope he found two copies of his own birth certificate. On one, his mother's name was listed as Lois Shirers, a name he didn't recognize, and in the space following his mother and father's names two words were stamped in square red letters. *Illegitimate Birth.* The second copy had been amended by Judge Westman, a man who ate his lunch each day at the café where the women worked. This copy included his mother's actual last name and was missing the red stamp.

Beneath the envelope he found another bundle of letters, these between Mildred and a member of Congress, a representative named Ralph Yarborough. Among the letters were other printed materials, resolutions, committee reports, and an affidavit signed by his grandmother and grandfather. In this bundle there was also a small stack of newspaper clippings. One was a photograph of his Aunt Suzy standing on the deck of a ship.

Another envelope held the marriage license of his grandparents. Carlos Frank Dews and Mildred Dorothea Scogin Dews.

Across the bottom of the trunk was a folded yellowing poster for a concert on the town square of Garrison. *Hank Williams and the Cowboys.*

Beneath the poster, inside a large white envelope, he found an even smaller envelope. It was an unopened letter from his grandmother, addressed to her brother Weldon in Korea. Over his address were stamped five words. *Recipient Deceased. Return to Sender.*

In another large white envelope, he found a single dollar bill. Next to the portrait of George Washington were two words. *Just wait.*

In the very bottom of the trunk, in a corner, wrapped in brown paper, Carlos found the rusted head of a double-edged ax.

1964

Lois sat on the hard, wooden pew at the back of the church. She looked beyond the open casket and stared at the curtain that covered the window of the baptismal pool. She hadn't been inside the red brick church in the center of Beaumont since her family had moved to Houston fifteen years before. And it had been eighteen years since he touched her and she followed him down the dark stairs into the water to be baptized.

The pews were crowded with members of the congregation and people stood at the back and along the aisles down the sides of the church. It was the largest crowd she had ever seen in the sanctuary. All for his funeral.

His widow sat in the center of the front pew. Lois moved her head from side to side to see the back of the woman's head, her white hair piled high on her head and her thin neck visible as she nodded acknowledgment to the guest preacher standing behind the pulpit. Lois wondered if she knew. What her husband had done, and what he had said to Lois on the day she was baptized. She wondered if she was the only girl he had touched that way. And she wondered, if he had, if he told them all that they were filled with sin, possessed by the devil, tempting men to sin.

Lois heard of his death by accident. As she refilled an early morning cup of a coffee for a regular customer at the café, she heard his name. The man in the booth asked his friend across the table if he had heard that the big preacher down in Beaumont, the one with the radio show, the one who had saved so many people, had died.

The man snapped the fold in the paper and handed it to his friend. He pointed to the headline. Lois looked over his shoulder at the paper.

As he walked out of the café after his breakfast the man dropped the paper into the wastebasket by the door. Lois walked to the door and took it from the basket. Behind the counter, she flattened the paper in front of her and read the obituary. Yes, he had died. The preacher who had touched her, told her of her evil, then baptized her into the church, had died. She stared at his photograph and read of his success, of the countless souls he had saved, and how many people he had reached via his weekly radio program. The funeral was scheduled for that afternoon. In his church. In the center of Beaumont.

Lois folded the paper, put it in her purse, and found Mildred in the kitchen.

"Mildred, I don't want you to ask me anything about it, but I need to take off from work the rest of the day. Maybe you can get one of the other girls to take my shift. I have to go down to Beaumont right now and I'm not sure what time I'll be back. It depends on the bus schedule."

"What do you mean, Lois? Is something wrong with one of your brothers?"

"I don't want to talk about it. It's just something I have to do. Please don't ask me to say anything else about it. I'll make up the shift later in the week. I'll try to be back tonight or tomorrow morning. Tell Mister Beal I'm sorry."

Lois walked home, changed into a dress, went to the bus station, and caught the next bus to Beaumont.

The preacher stood at the pulpit behind the coffin. He asked those in the church who had been baptized by Brother Williams to stand. More than half of the people in the sanctuary stood. Lois remained in her seat. She looked around at the women who were standing.

There were others like her there, others he had touched, others he had told they were the source of evil, full of the devil. She could tell.

The members of the congregation sat back down and Lois watched them. The others like her, with their heads hanging down, tight expressions on their faces, hard lines on their foreheads, the cast of shame around their eyes. They had stooped shoulders and they crossed their hands nervously in their laps. She recognized them because they looked the way she had looked for so long whenever she saw herself in a mirror. She wondered if others had seen her the way she saw these women now. She knew she didn't want to become one of them.

Lois didn't know why she was there, what she hoped to accomplish by taking the bus to Beaumont and walking through the city's streets to find this red brick church with its tall white steeple, filled with people professing their love and grief for a man responsible for her years of shame and fear.

As the preacher continued to speak of the many virtues of Brother Williams, Lois considered what she might do. She could go to the cemetery and kick dirt on his coffin, or she could spit on his grave. She could talk to his wife and tell her what he had done to her and other girls like her. She could interrupt the service and shout to the congregation what he had done to her all those years before. But now, sitting in the pew, surrounded by his congregation, none of these seemed right.

Since Carlos had left her thirteen years before, at the curb at the end of the driveway that led to the little house where she found Suzy and Mildred, Lois had learned a few things for sure.

She knew that shame was worthless. She had spent years walking through town and working through her shifts feeling the eyes of everyone on her. She was convinced that everyone who saw her knew of her guilt, knew that her baby's father wouldn't have her, knew of her shame, knew that she had a bastard child, that she was a sinner and had given in to the devil and his call. But that shame had slowly melted away.

When she first started working at the café, Mister Beal told Mildred to tell Lois to start looking people in the eyes when she took their orders. He had noticed that she stared at the table in front of them as she wrote their orders on her little green and white lined pad. She knew that they knew her story and couldn't face the judgment in their eyes. Now, she could look any man or woman in the face and not feel judged.

Living in the little house with Mildred and Suzy and raising their boy together, she had learned that love was more important than shame, that shame had been invented to make people feel bad about doing things they truly wanted to do or couldn't help but do. She knew that the goodness she saw in her boy each day was more important than a stamp on a birth certificate or whether the boy had a father he could call daddy. She wanted him to be proud of himself, with or without a father to claim him. And she wanted him to be proud of her.

She knew that there was no evil, or that evil was simply a matter of opinion. She saw more bad things done by men trying to outrun what had been called evil than by the thing called evil. All the heartache and pain that she, Mildred, and Suzy had faced seemed to come from men doing bad things but blaming women for them all.

And she knew that there wasn't a God, at least the kind the preachers spoke about. The only faith she had was in what she believed she could see and feel for herself. The only faith she had was in good people doing what was right, not what was written in a book by men and then read out and explained to a congregation by other men.

The funeral service ended with a hymn and the preacher asked all those in the congregation to file by the open coffin to say goodbye to the righteous man who had led them for the past thirty years. Lois stood and waited her turn.

She paused in front of the polished wood coffin. They had dressed him in a black suit, white shirt, and black tie. He was thin;

his brown hair, now white, was slicked back and across his head. His face was shrunken, his cheekbones made points beneath the corners of his eyes. He looked frail and pinched.

Lois felt pity for this old feeble man. She would never know why he did what he did, what made him want to touch girls that way, what he gained from teaching girls that they were evil and then offering his salvation to them. But she knew, even if he were still alive, that he couldn't harm her now. She had changed, even if he had stayed the same. She was no longer the vulnerable girl on her knees and shivering in the small room above the baptismal pool.

Her desire to walk away and leave behind any remaining hatred or pain was now stronger than any desire for revenge. She reached out and touched the white satin lining of his coffin. She found pleasure in the cool slick cloth. She turned and walked back down the aisle of the church.

She was free. Her life was simple and her daily worries were few. She didn't have a man in her life and didn't want one. She had a good job, Mildred, and the boy. They were enough. It would be enough. And it wasn't evil. She wasn't evil. She was without shame.

Lois walked down the steps of the church and toward the bus station. She sat behind the driver as the bus drove north toward Nacogdoches. She passed the time by singing songs to herself, under her breath, with her eyes closed.

"Just as I am, without one plea, but that thy blood was shed for me, and that thou bidd'st me come to thee, O Lamb of God, I come, I come."

1964

Carlos sat in silence as his grandfather drove the pickup truck through the streets of Nacogdoches and out into the rolling hills north of town. The man's gray felt cowboy hat sat on the seat between them.

Carlos had never been alone with his grandfather and had only known the man for two months. He avoided looking at him, staring at his own feet on the floorboard of the truck or looking out the side window. When a car or truck came up behind them, the old man edged the truck onto the shoulder and let it pass. They were on their way to the man's farm in the country.

"Sugar, you keep working, Granny'll see who that is at the door."

When his grandfather had knocked on the front door of their little house two months before, Carlos sat at the kitchen table writing a story. His grandmother stood at the sink washing dishes. Mildred dried her hands with a dish towel as she walked to the front door.

Her husband stood with his right hand on the door frame for support and almost fell into the room when Mildred opened the door. He was stick-thin, and his knees shook as he tried to keep his balance. His eyes were blood-red, his face wet with tears. A trail of drool dropped from his chin to the bib of his overalls. All he could say was her name before he collapsed into her arms. She caught him and helped him into the house and to the sofa.

Mildred agreed that day to take him in. He had surrendered to the cancer, his fate, and to her. Like a child, he would follow the rules of her house and she would take care of him until the end.

When he came to stay with them in the little house on Raquet Street, he got up every morning, folded and put away the quilt he used for cover, and straightened the sofa where he slept. He dressed in his overalls and boots and went to his place in the country to tend to his cattle, or to have coffee with men he knew who came into town to the feed or hardware stores. But as the weeks passed, he could only make it to the carport to sit in the porch swing. In the last week, he had only made it to a chair in the kitchen before he dropped down, exhausted and in pain. He sat for hours on the toilet. Carlos could hear his grandfather crying through the bathroom door.

"Son, I want you to see where I'm turning off the highway here, so you can remember it."

The man slowed the pickup and pushed down the turn signal to indicate a left turn. "See this little road here? This little place is the Fitzy junction, and this road goes out to my place. Your granny grew up just down the road here a piece. This turn is halfway between Nacogdoches and Garrison." He waited for an oncoming truck to pass and turned down the sandy road that ran between houses, with fenced cow meadows and small gardens beside and behind them. "I want you to be able to find the place if you ever need to on your own."

The boy looked at the houses and trees and the look of the road to mark the spot.

They drove through hay meadows and stands of pine trees planted in perfect rows to the crest of a high hill, sloping down into dark woods along a creek. "This is the Naconiche Creek. That's an Indian name. Like Nacogdoches. This creek runs cool clear water all year, no matter how little rain we get. It runs and twists around through the woods till it comes across the back of my place. It's the line between my place and the Hayes place."

The truck climbed up from the creek bottom and passed through fields of grazing cattle and stands of tall pines. The red sand road was only wide enough for a single vehicle. Weeds grew along the road and brushed against the sides of the truck. When the man saw another car coming toward them he pulled to the side of the road and waited for it to squeeze by. He lifted his fingers from the steering wheel to wave, nodded his head, and mouthed the word howdy.

"Now, Sugar, Granny wants you to do this for her."

Carlos had run back to his room when he heard his grandfather ask his grandmother and mother if he might go with him out to his place in the country. The man had said it might be the last time he could make the trip, and he wanted to see the place and feed his cows one more time.

The boy sat on his bed with his grandmother on her knees in front of him. She held his hands between hers. "Your granddaddy is mighty weak. You can see that. He'll be dying real soon. The cancer's almost got him. And he needs your help. He says you can help him open the gates and pitch down bales of hay out of the barn to give to the cows. What if he got out there and something happened to him? He'd have no way of getting to any help, now would he? Will you do this just for Granny? This one time?"

The boy nodded and they went back to the living room together.

Later, Carlos turned back toward the front of the little house as he and his grandfather walked to the truck parked on the street. His mother held the screen door open against the pull of its spring and stood on the threshold. His grandmother stood just in front of her on the single brick step down onto the concrete walk.

"This place we are going to is still called the Nall's place. The man I used to work for was Mister Hart and Mister Hart's wife was a Nall. He helped me get the place. Talked to Mister Nall, who let me pay for it over time. I done worked like a dog saving the money for it. Maybe it'll be called the Dews place someday. But for now, it's called the Nall's place."

The man turned down a narrower road that passed between two fields and disappeared into distant woods. "This road here goes in-between these two places, the Stanaland place here on the right and the Clifton place here on the left. The only place this road goes is down to my place, and I like it that way. No other houses too close either. No near neighbors means no trouble."

The fields beside the road ended as they drove into a stand of hardwood and pine trees. The trees formed a tunnel of green, and the bright sun disappeared behind them. In the distance, Carlos saw a small opening of light. After a quarter mile in the dark woods, the truck came to a gate. Beyond it, a field opened in front of them. The man stopped the truck with the front grill almost touching the rusted steel tubes of the gate. He took a key from the truck's ashtray. "Son, take this key, unlock the gate. Leave the lock hanging on the chain. You don't need to lock it back behind us. Open the gate, and close it behind me after I drive through. If the gate drags on the ground and gets stuck, just lift up on it, it'll open. You're strong enough to pick it up. I told your granny you would help me with this heavy gate and save me the straining and pain."

The boy opened the gate and his grandfather drove through. He closed the gate and climbed back into the cab of the pickup. They drove into the field and passed a small weathered farmhouse.

"When your granny left me, I saved every penny I could get my hands on to buy this little place. Only twenty-six acres, but big enough. Bought me some cows of my own, fixed up that little house, and been set ever since. Nobody to answer to, and any money from off the place at the end of the year is all mine. No more working on the halves and doing what another man wants me to do. The little house was here when I bought the place, but it was fallin in. I fixed it up enough for me and your daddy to live in. Still using the old out-house in the back. Had a deep well dug, and now I've got the sweet-est water in the county."

The man breathed deeply and his voice strengthened. "There's no place I'd rather be in this world than out here on this old place. I'm the first man in the family for as far back as anyone can remember to own any property. I just like to walk around and feel the grass and dirt under my boots and know I own it all. If this cancer hadn't got me, I'd have been able to get even more land, and more head of cattle too."

The man steered the pickup off the road through the pasture toward a small stock pond in the back of the field.

"Before we feed the cows, I got something I want us to do together." He drove to the side of the pond near the edge of the stand of trees that bordered the field. "There's a sapling oak here at the edge of these woods. I want you to help me reach up and pull the top down."

He winced as he stepped from the truck. He lifted the back of the truck's seat and removed a thick, crooked walking stick, then stepped to the bed of the truck and lifted an ax from under a feed sack.

"Son, I want you to take this walking stick and reach up as high as you can and hook the top of this little oak here. When you get it pulled down, I'll grab hold of it and pull it down far enough to cut."

Carlos took the stick, held it at the straight end, and stood at the base of the small tree. He hooked its upper fork with the bend of the stick and pulled it down. The young tree bent, and Carlos stepped away from it to bring the very top within his grandfather's reach.

"We need to be careful not to bend it too sharp, or it'll snap on down the trunk."

The old man moaned as he stretched up and took the walking stick from the boy's hands. He brought the top of the tree down level with his chest. "I got it now, so you step back."

The man gripped the ax handle near the head and, with two chops, cut off the top four feet of the tree. He dropped the ax to the ground and held the top of the tree with his hand as he removed the crook of the walking stick. He let go of the tree, letting it snap upward. The boy walked to his side and they stood looking at the tree, awkward and squat, missing its upper branches.

"Topping that tree like that will make it fork at the top and make it easy to recognize."

The man picked up the top of the tree and put it in the bed of the pickup. "You'll probably end up with this place. My boy sure won't be getting it. So when this place is yours, you can come back here and look at this forked old tree, think back and remember this day I brung you out here and did this. That way you'll remember the old sick man who left you this place. You know you are the only son of an only son of an only son?"

"Yes, sir."

"There only been one of us Dews men in each generation. And the last three of us have had the name of Carlos. Your granny always said that the world could only handle one Dews man at a time." The man walked to Carlos's side and rested his hand on the boy's shoulder. "Now, let's go put out some hay for them cows."

As they drove toward the barn, the man blew the horn of the truck in short bursts. "I use the horn to call up my cows. They know it means they are fixin to be fed. See em coming toward us from across the pasture?"

They parked at the side of the large gray barn in the center of the pasture. A plank lot surrounded it. "Before we get out of the pickup, I wanna warn you about that bull coming yonder. These cows are gentle as can be, but you need to watch out for that old bull. He can be mean sometimes. And your granny would never forgive me if I let anything happen to you while you were out here on the place with me. Now, see him? He's the white one with the black face and the big old hump on his back. See those big old horns? You don't want to mess with him."

The boy watched as the bull used his horns to push aside the cows that got in his way as they walked toward the barn.

"I sure am proud of that bull. But he is just about too much for me now. He is registered and everything. A Bremmer. I've got the papers on him there in the glove box of the pickup too. But he can be a mean son of a bitch. Let's slip on into the barn before he gets all the way here."

They entered the barn through a small door cut into its side. Except for the few churches and basketball gyms he had been in,

Carlos had never been inside such a large building. It was half full of hay, stacked all the way to the high rafters.

"I want you to climb up to the top of the hay and throw down eight bales. I'll give you my pocket knife and I want you to cut the strings around the bales. I want you to carry the hay in bunches and pitch it over into those hay racks along that side wall. Spread it out so you fill the whole rack. When you're done, I'll turn the cows into the lot so they can come in this hall along the side of the barn and eat the hay."

Carlos climbed to the top of the stack of hay and threw down the first bale.

"You are just like a monkey, climbing up on that stack of hay. I sure wish I had had you to help me out here for the past few years. You look plenty strong enough. I'm gonna sit out here and rest on the tailgate of the pickup while you put out that hay. You come and get me when you're done." He walked out the small door and closed it behind him.

Carlos threw down the bales, hearing the chuff of the taut strings as he cut them and the bales expanded. He carried armloads of the hay to each section of the rack until all the bales were gone, and the rack was filled with the sweet dusty hay.

When he was done, Carlos walked out of the small side door of the barn. His grandfather sat back against the lowered tailgate of the truck. The man's feet were wide apart and his penis hung from the open fly of his overalls. His head was bowed and his eyes were closed.

"I'm finished with the hay."

The man opened his eyes and looked up at the boy. "Son, that came out of me."

His grandfather's eyes moved to the ground in front of him. Carlos followed his gaze. On the ground in the space between his grandfather's boots, the boy saw a small mound of clotted blood and flesh. Pink, gray, deep purple, and white. There were a few drops of blood and a clear fluid on the side of the man's boots.

Carlos looked to his grandfather's face. The man appeared sickened and shook his head in disgust at the sight between his boots.

"Boy oh boy, them doctors down there sure did mess me up. They say they ground my bladder too thin trying to get all that cancer out of me. Now I'm just sluffing off all that blood and scabs and chunks of cancer out of my peter."

He paused and took a deep breath. His voice broke. "I won't be around much longer, and I sure don't want to die down there in town. I asked your granny to move out here to the place with me, but she said no. I guess I'll die in a little room in the middle of town. Sometimes I wish I could just curl up in the soft pine straw under them trees and die right there. Just close my eyes, go to sleep, and not wake up. I'm ready."

The old man removed a handkerchief from the front of his overalls and wiped blood from the tip of his penis, tucked it back inside his overalls, and buttoned them. He used the toe of his boot to cover the blood and flesh between his feet with grass and dirt. He cleared his throat and swallowed. "Let's turn them cows in on that hay."

Carlos and his grandfather walked to the side of the lot. "You climb up to the top of the fence and watch as I open the gate and let em in. They sure look hungry, don't they?"

The old man walked to the opposite side of the lot where the cows had gathered at the wide gate. He opened it and the cows crowded in, making their way through the lot toward the hallway with the hay. The big white bull pushed in among the cows, scattering them, swinging his head and sharp horns to make way for himself. The bull was first down the hallway toward the hay. He rushed after him and closed the gate, trapping the bull in the hallway by himself.

"I decided to trap that damned bull in there by himself," he said, walking back to where Carlos stood. "Look at the big sore on the side of that heifer. That damned bull has got her with one of his horns. It looks like he almost tore her guts out. And it's fresh. Must have done it in the past day or two."

Carlos looked to where the man pointed. A red cow with a stark white face stood against the fence of the lot. Just behind her left shoulder he saw a red gash, almost a foot long, bordered in white with black scabs forming across it.

"I caught him in there with the hay by himself. I better get rid of him before he kills one of them. As much I like him and am proud of him, I don't think I can handle him anymore, and he sure is hurting them heifers. Mister Clifton, the man who has been feeding the cows for me, told me he would sell him for me if I could pen him in that chute. He's scared of him too and doesn't want to try to catch him. If we can get him in the loading chute, Mister Clifton and his boy can come down here with his truck and trailer, load the mean bastard, and take him to the auction house down in Nacogdoches tomorrow. I'm gonna let all of the cows and calves back out of the lot. They can eat their hay later. If I let him go from the hall into the lot but open up the little loading chute gate, he'll try to get out that way, and I can close the gate of the chute and catch him up in there. You stand right outside the lot by the gate to the hall. See this nail in this piece of wood? When I tell you to, you pull it toward you. The gate'll swing open and he'll try to get out of the lot to the cows."

The man walked into the lot and, waving his arms, shooed the cows back out into the pasture. He closed the wide gate and walked in the lot back toward Carlos.

"Now, you wait till I get behind that little gate at the end of the loading chute. I'll hide behind it, and when he goes down it to get out I'll close the gate behind him and trap him in it. He's mad enough being caught up in that pen and separated from them cows that there's no telling what he would do to me if he caught me in that lot alone. You understand, right? Don't you, Son?"

The man and the boy exchanged nods.

Carlos looked between the planks of the lot fence and into the small enclosure. The bull snorted and shook his head. Carlos looked down at the nail he was to pull to open the small gate, once his grandfather was safely behind the other gate across the lot.

His grandfather began walking across the dusty lot. The bull snorted again and stepped toward the gate.

Carlos pulled on the nail and the gate swung open, his grandfather in the middle of the open lot.

The bull rushed out toward him.

Carlos lowered his head so that the weathered wood of the fence blocked his view into the lot. He heard the rush of the heavy bull, a single snort, and a blunt thud.

The boy waited in silence, his hand still on the nail driven into the gate latch.

He took a step to his left and looked between two planks into the lot. A small cloud of dust rose around the bull.

His grandfather was face down, his arms out to his sides. His legs, between the front hooves of the bull, were crossed at the ankle. The bull lowered its head and brushed its wet nose against the blue fabric of the back of the man's overalls.

The man didn't move.

Carlos counted to ten and looked inside the lot again. His grandfather hadn't moved. The bull shoved the man's body with its thick black horns.

Carlos turned and walked away.

He passed his grandfather's truck, walked beside the little house at the edge of the field and to the gate. He walked through it and locked it behind him, dropping the heavy keys into his pocket.

He stopped at the edge of the woods, bent down, and tied the laces of his right shoe, using the special knot his grandmother taught him how to tie.

The road through the woods would take him to the home of a neighbor who would call his grandmother at the café. His mother and grandmother would come and get him. They would take him home. They would ask him what happened. And he would tell them the first story of his own.

CPSIA information can be obtained
at www.ICGtesting.com
Printed in the USA
LVHW090125131020
668647LV00005B/32/J